FLICKERING FLAMES

This is the oldest picture of a lamp so far discovered. It is a
seventh- or eighth-century manuscript illumination. The lamp
seems to have three stiff wicks, which could be papyrus stalks.

FLICKERING FLAMES

A History of Domestic Lighting through the Ages

by Leroy Thwing
Former Editor of "The Rushlight"

Published for the Rushlight Club

CHARLES E. TUTTLE COMPANY
Rutland, Vermont

Representatives
Continental Europe: BOXERBOOKS, INC., *Zurich*
British Isles: PRENTICE-HALL INTERNATIONAL, INC., *London*
Australasia: PAUL FLESCH & CO., PTY. LTD., *Melbourne*
Canada: M. G. HURTIG LTD., *Edmonton*

Published by the
Charles E. Tuttle Company, Inc.
of Rutland, Vermont & Tokyo, Japan
with editorial offices at
Suido 1-chome, 2-6, Bunkyo-ku, Tokyo

Copyright in Japan, 1958 by Charles E. Tuttle Co., Inc.

Library of Congress Catalog Card
No. 57–12287

International Standard Book No. 0-8048-0185-1

First edition, 1958
Tenth printing, 1972

Book design, layout, & typography by
Roland A. Mulhauser

Printed in Japan

Contents

Acknowledgments

The author acknowledges his indebtedness to the files of *The Rushlight*, quarterly bulletin of the Rushlight Club, and to the members of the Club who have contributed to it during the past twenty-five years. He is especially grateful to Professor Edwin B. Rollins, its former editor, to Mrs. Lura Woodside Watkins and to several others for articles in *The Rushlight* which have been adapted for this book. These articles are included in the bibliography. Further acknowledgement is due Professor Quentin L. Coons for his untiring efforts in facilitating tne publication of this volume.

Leroy Thwing

Cambridge, Mass.

Introduction

"Early lighting" suggests the use of candles and whale oil lamps, but these mark neither the beginning nor the end of the history of artificial illumination. The story begins in prehistoric times; the story of lamps ends when kerosene and gas were superseded by the electric current. At this point lighting enters a new phase, with new principles and new methods which are outside the scope of this book.

Within the limits stated, lighting may be roughly divided into four periods—the period of primitive methods, the Classical period, the Medieval period, and the period of invention. No sharply defined boundary separates one period from another; rather there is a gradual transition, with much overlapping, governed by conditions having no direct connection with lighting and yet indirectly hindering or advancing its development.

Primitive methods are those of people of limited knowledge or resources. Prehistoric man is supposed to have first relied upon a flaming brand from his campfire for a portable light, and by accident or experience to have devised a better torch and a simple lamp, possibly a shell holding grease or pitch with a wick of moss. Means available to individuals, rather than a particular time, determined the continued use of primitive methods, with the result that lamps of the simplest type have been found in use in all ages.

The Classical period is thought of as that which covers the best of the Greek and Roman civilizations, although these drew from earlier cultures of Egypt and the Near East. In a time of rivalry for the control of the then known world, it saw the treasures of the weak carried away by the strong, the rise of great cities enriched by trade and conquest, and the palaces of the wealthy abounding in the best that skilled craftsmanship afforded, including lamps of great beauty, although these were hardly more effective than the humbler utensils of the poor. This period ended when Roman supremacy declined and its wealth and luxury were swept away.

In sharp contrast with the splendor of the Classical period was the desolation and poverty of the five centuries from 500 to 1000 A.D., the Dark Ages, when savage peoples from the Continent overran England, then abandoned by the Romans, while Teutonic barbarians swept over all Roman provinces, even into Italy, and Moors from Africa occupied the Spanish peninsula and a part of France. Much of the former progress was lost and it is little to be wondered at that lighting reached a low ebb and the pine torch and hearth fire sufficed for the mead halls of the northern warriors and the rude huts of their followers.

The five hundred years ending with the discovery of America by Columbus saw the invasion of England by the Normans in 1066, the Crusades (1096–1273), the rise and decline of Feudalism and, with the spread of Christianity, the establishment of schools and monasteries. All these had notable influence and once more an atmosphere prevailed in which industry and the pursuit of knowledge could flourish. The Norman invasion dotted England with the castles of the Norman nobles and the substantial manor houses of their vassals. Records are few to tell of the lighting of these homes, but old-time illustrations and accounts show the use of candles on the table, servants holding torches in the banquet hall, and suspended candle-beams.

The poorer classes had little need for artificial light, since their life was one of labor from sun to sun, and a fire-pan or fatted rush furnished all the light needed.

The Crusades broadened the outlook of the people of western Europe and led to trade which brought in the luxury goods of far away places, including lighting devices of copper, brass and pottery.

The feudal system made possible the magnificent chateaux of France, embellished with fine ironwork for which the workmen of the Middle Ages were famous. They created ornamental and useful lanterns and candle fixtures.

With the spread of Christianity into northwestern Europe came the twelfth-century enthusiasm for building cathedrals. Skilled craftsmen made their candelabra, sanctuary lamps and coronas, of which the Hildesheim corona is a famous example. Kings and nobles gave beautiful lamps to the churches as votive offerings, and trade guilds established foundations for maintaining lights before the shrines of their patron saints.

Colonial America relied upon the pine splint (candle-wood), grease and heavy-oil lamps, and candles. The better lamps were imported until the mid-sixteen hundreds. Lamps for burning whale oil were made of brass and pewter, as well as tin, and, about 1800, of glass. Such was the interest in improved lighting that in the fifty years subsequent to 1800 over 500 American patents were granted for improvements in lighting devices. The era of lamp improvement began with the work of Miles and Argand in the late 1780's; Miles with a non-spillable lamp with vertical wick-tube, and Argand with an improved burner employing a new principle for ensuring better combustion of the fuel and a brighter light.

Fuels, too, received attention. Olive oil held its long established place in regions around the Mediterranean; but other oils, vegetable, fish and whale oils, fed the lamps of

Europe and America for many years. For economic reasons whale oil gave way to lard oil in the first half of the eighteenth century, and for a time had some competition from burning fluids made of alcohol and turpentine.

Candle materials profited from new knowledge in the field of chemistry and the soft, greasy tallow became stearine and stearic acid, the basis of the best modern candles.

Gas made by distillation of coal entered the lighting field in the early 1800's and met with favor until displaced by the electric light.

Kerosene took precedence over the heavier oils after the discovery of petroleum in Pennsylvania. With it came new designs of lamps and burners suited to this more volatile material, and with them lighting by flame lamps reached its peak.

Edwin B. Rollins

Publisher's Note

No attempt is made in this book to describe the lamps used in Eastern Europe and Asia. So far as observed these are technically similar to those used in Italy, Switzerland, Austria and Western Europe, although their outward forms are different.

FLICKERING FLAMES

Early Lighting Devices

The story of artificial lighting is older than history for it begins with the first man-made fire. Open fires and burning branches were the first fixed and portable lights. Torches are doubtless as old as the roughly-chipped stone axes of the Old Stone Age.

Devices to hold burning wood came later. Homer mentions bowls filled with blazing faggots. The Pharos at Alexandria, one of the seven wonders of the ancient world, was lighted by a wood fire as other lighthouses were for a thousand years afterwards—the beacon on Beacon Hill in Boston was a wood-burning fire basket.

Although wood-burning techniques are oldest of all, lamps are known to be products of the Old Stone Age; before man learned to shape the crudest pottery or weave the simplest fabric he had made a lamp. Though progress was not equal everywhere, the occupants of a cave in France have left us a sandstone lamp used some 20,000 years ago. Found with hardened grease and vegetable fiber still in it, this lamp has on the bottom the incised figure of a deer. A replica, with moss for a wick and candle grease for fuel, burns very well indeed (Plate 21).

By the time there was anything like history, stone and shell lamps had been supplanted by similar lamps made of clay. The development of these lamps in the Mediterranean area and the Near East is covered in several well-illustrated books by prominent archeologists and will be but briefly discussed here. The classical lamp at its best was an end product; nothing seems to have developed from it except possibly spout lamps. Romans carried their lamps into Britain and Gaul but, after the so-called Fall of Rome, they fell into disuse and others more suited to northern conditions were developed.

Classical Lamps

Pottery lamps of either sun-dried or baked clay were the common lights of antiquity. The first written description of them is found in Herodotus, who wrote about 450 B. C. He said that at the Feast of Sais in Egypt lamps filled with oil, to which salt had been added, were carried in the procession. The tall handsome alabaster lamps found in King Tut-Ankh-Amen's tomb are much older and some simpler type of lamp may well have been used in his time but there is no present evidence of it. With the possible exception of these float lamps, the contribution of Egyptian civilization to the art of illumination was slight. In Greece and Rome pottery lamps sufficed for the poorer classes, while the homes of the patricians were lighted by the more durable bronze lamps. But with all their skill as artists and artisans, Greek and Roman lamp makers never discovered those principles of combustion which produce brighter lights. They increased the number of wicks, but the smoke and odor was proportionately great until, as a Greek writer records, "One could not enjoy the good things of the table until indulgence in wine made the guests indifferent to the smoking lamps." At a time when the testing of a theory by experiment was thought unprofessional and undignified, it is not surprising that their only progress was in improving the appearance by graceful design and artistic decoration.

2

There is, however, some evidence of technical improvement. A small bronze lamp, presumed to be at least fifteen hundred years old was dug up in the old marketplace in Athens. This has a wick support—a nearly complete tube—of which we have no other example until the fifteenth century. This is one of the many improvements and inventions that have lain dormant until conditions were more favorable for their use. The Greek engineer Heron (c. 200 B.C.) described a device for adjusting the wick of a saucer-type lamp automatically and there are other inventions for supplying oil to the wick either by water pressure or by a vacuum (actually by air pressure). The first was tried again in the early nineteenth century but without considerable success; the second, however, was adopted by Cardan in the sixteenth century and later by Argand.

Those interested in classical lamps should consult Broneer, the lamp catalogs of the British and the Victoria Museums, also many other archeological publications.

Wood-Burning Utensils

It is evident that the first domestic lights were faggots or branches of burning wood used without bowls, baskets or other holding devices. Burning branches were improved by splitting wood into smaller strips and binding them together. These were the first torches and, much later, torch holders of the type seen on the Statue of Liberty were devised as a protection against falling sparks. The art of the torch-maker is a very old one and has persisted through Medieval and Victorian times down to the present—even in the United States. The wooden splint, a long sliver of wood, is a refinement of the torch for domestic use. Two examples of their use are given below.

The following is taken from an English translation (1658) of Olaus Magnus' *History of the Goths*, 1555; the author was Archbishop of Upsala, one of the oldest cities in Sweden:

"The North People being used to most long nights, use divers kinds of lights. Most people who live under the North Pole use the fat of sea monsters in winter to do all their occasions. This fat when put into lamps shines most clearly and largely. Moreover in all the North they use pine-tree torches that have natural pitch upon them and also candles of pine, finely split, which they hold under their belts or their hats or in their mouths, and thus they walk as they please, vexed by no blasts of wind. Such candles are sometimes as long as their arms, according to the length of the night. The fat of sea monsters they put a wick to. The fat of the whale is much in the body but greatest in the head. Sometimes there are 30 to 40 flagons of it, where of a man can scarcely carry a single one. This oil poured into lamps and always added unto, will burn continuously before an Altar or other sacred place both night and day."

From P.A. Beilstein, Petrograd, 1907, *Splints and Splint-ho.ders in Lat ia:*

"The splintholder is an old Lettish utensil; its origin is prehistoric. In my youth I have seen farmers sit around a burning splint to spin or work at other household tasks. The rough plank floor was pitted with holes burned by the glowing coals which dropped from the splint. A burning splint guided a man to the horses or a woman to the cows. These splints were made of birch, split

4

from logs about three feet long, which had been dried behind the oven. Pitch pine and fir were also used but only the heart wood is suitable.

"Fear of fire and the need for some sort of a support stimulated the development of a splintholder with jaws or a grip into which the down-sloping splint could be thrust. Some stood on the table, others on the floor. Some were entirely of wood and others of iron or at least with iron grips. Others had a hook for suspension from a beam.

"The threshing room had a clay floor. About three feet above this in a corner was a sort of grate, whose wooden bars were overlaid with flat stones, on which a small fire burned. Projecting from the wall was a splint holder gripping two splints whose burning ends were over the fire, which not only received the dropping coals but helped the splints to burn. On the floor a log separated the threshing floor from the fire area. Above, a sort of wooden hood thickly smeared with clay served as a protection from floating chaff."

Splint holders are of two types depending on the kind of wood to be burned in them. Birchwood splints, which have no pitch, must be burned in a horizontal or down-sloping position, as may be seen in Plate 1. Pitchy woods, such as pine and fir, will burn at an angle of 45 degrees and sometimes nearly erect, varying with the amount of pitch in the splint. There are several types of holders depending on the kind of wood burned and also on the place of their origin. Splint holders of the inverted pincer type seem to have been used more in the British Isles than on the Continent. Von Benesch shows many of the spring fork type and others, but few of the pincer type, although it seems likely that they were used. Note the small fire pans and

5

baskets in the above plate, in Plate 2, and also the splint holders in Plate 23.

There is objective proof of the use of fork-type holders as early as 500 B.C. In the United States National Museum and elsewhere there are tall bronze standards with three cleft arms at the top. These are sometimes called candelabra but they were not made to hold candles but lights. These lights were splints as is clearly shown in a mural at Orvieto in Italy. The pertinent part of this is shown in Plate 22. It is apparent that the three burning objects are thin slivers of wood, as their thickness at different angles has been accurately delineated by the artist.

An elderly Russian on being asked what kind of lights they had in his home when he was a boy replied, " Bits of sticks." This is what the first settlers in New England found the Indians using. We have the testimony of a clergyman and a colonial governor for this. The Reverend Master Higginson wrote in 1630 from Salem " (Splints) are made of the wood of the pine tree, cloven in little slices, something thin, which are so full of turpentine that they burn as clear as a torch." William Wood, however, who commented on them a few years later, was more critical. He " could not commend it as it is something sluttish, dropping a sort of pitchie substance where it stands." Although the use of splints seems to have been common in some parts of Scotland and Ireland, they must have been relatively unknown in southern England for they were a curiosity to Governor Winthrop of Connecticut and he sent specimens of candlewood to the Royal Society.

Candlewood is the New England word for splints. There is ample evidence that it was much sought after during the early part of the eighteenth century, although not necessarily for lights, for large quantities were used for kindling wood, ror tar products and by charcoal burners. (See Judd's

6

History of Hadley.) There is no convincing evidence that New Englanders ever used it for lighting purposes except possibly to burn in fire pans. There is almost no evidence that they ever burned it in splint holders. They may have carried splints in their hands as the Swedes did. Fire pans, cressets and fire baskets are mentioned in colonial documents but not splint holders.

Splint holders of the inverted tongs type are rare. They differ from rushlight holders only in size. One in a local collection is about four feet tall and weighs eighteen pounds. The pincers are 1½ inches wide and ¼ inch thick (Plate 9). One can imagine it standing in a blacksmith's shop, where the smoke from a sliver of pitchwood would not be noticed. If there are any splint holders of New England provenance, they are likely to have been brought here by the Scotch or made here by them. There is an abundance of pitchy pine and bog fir in Scotland, where it was burned in a "puirman", the local name for a splint holder. Pine knots were burned in cresset stones.

A cresset is a small fire basket—usually portable. John Gower, the fourteenth century poet says, " There was a pot of earth in which he hath a light brennying in a cresset. " John Stow in his *Survey of London* (1598) says, "Every constable in London had his cresset and one to bear it, and one to have a light in a bag and serve it ". Two cressets are mentioned in an Essex County cooper's will and they were used on the landing stages along the Mississippi in Mark Twain's day. The cressets illustrated in Plate 2 are of Continental origin but these forms are doubtless universal. One illustrated in *Life on the Mississippi* is basket-shaped and supported on a pole.

The use of burning wood for illumination is the oldest form of lighting and it has been used ever since, as the following letter printed in the June 1936 *Rushlight* proves:

7

"In many parts of the South 'lightwood' is still used, particularly by the colored people who burn chunks of this in the fireplace both for heat and light. It is also used for hunting 'possums and 'coons at night. The torch is a bundle of several splinters of lightwood about the size of the finger; when well-lighted they will not blow out and they burn with a bright flame lasting as long as an hour, depending on the length of the splinters. In the pitch pine belt there still remains, either in the stumps or in dead trees, some of the original growth. Real lightwood is found only in the heartwood of these dead trees. It is a deep yellow or light brown color and is very heavy. When lighted it burns with a sizzling flame and thick, oily black smoke, which has an unmistakably fragrant odor."

Discoveries by French archaeologists have shown that the oil lamp was in use at the close of the Bronze Age (c. 10,000 B. C.) among the prehistoric lake dwellers of Switzerland. According to Dr. Hough these are the most ancient objects which have been found so far that are unmistakably lamps.

—J. D.

Medieval Lighting

We know little, except in a general way, about domestic lighting during the thousand years following the so-called Fall of the Roman Empire. We can assume that the warmer Mediterranean countries continued to use the same lamps they had been using, but these were not suited for colder countries where the olive tree does not flourish. We know almost nothing except by speculation and deduction about the lighting devices used in Central Europe during the Dark Ages and very little more about them during the Middle Ages. Doubtless there were wood-burning devices, torches, crude candles and simple lamps, always depending on the light-producing materials available in any particular locality. It can be reasonably assumed that the classical type of clay lamp, burning a liquid fuel, was not used in colder countries such as France, Germany and Austria, where the only illuminant was some kind of animal fat, for which different lamps had to be developed. It appears that metal grease-burning lamps developed in Central Europe during the above millenium. There is no hard proof of this but it is a reasonable assumption that the lamps used as late as 1700 differ little from those used in the year 1000. Such lamps we now call grease, pan and saucer lamps. Wick support lamps were a great improvement and may have appeared about 1400. Grease lamps are no more than metal replicas of the caveman's stone lamp and the simplest clay utensils of early historical times, although they were developed independently. If we had a number of these tenth- to fourteenth-century lamps, there would be no way of proving them to be such, by inspection, as their design seems to have changed so very little over a long period of time.

It is usually impossible by inspection alone to be sure how old any simple, common household utensil is, if it is older than printed books or any kind of pictures. Household devices excavated at Herculaneum are dated by events but we must usually depend on words and pictures. The oldest description of a lighting device is over 3000 years old and it is, so to speak, still in print. This is the description in the Book of Exodus of the great golden "candlestick" or lampholder—the Menorah—made for the first Jewish tabernacle by Bezaleel. Unfortunately for our special interest, it is the stand or holder that is described in great detail, not the lamps. There are few early miniatures depicting the float lamps hung in sanctuaries from the earliest Christian times. There is a fifteenth-century series of engravings showing the five wise and the five foolish virgins, each carrying a large float lamp. Thus we know that float lamps were used in medieval times but as they required oil, it is doubtful if they were used in the North except in churches. If they were, we would be unable to identify them, since a float lamp can be made from any saucer or bowl-shaped vessel. Fortunately we have one or more sixteenth-century pictures of a contemporary lamp. It is shown as a detail in one of the plates in Besson's *Theatrum Machinorum* (1568). (See Plate 24.) A similar lamp is depicted in one of Rembrandt's engravings. One was excavated in Roman-occupied Britain some years ago. But are these cast brass lamps typical of the lamps used in the average home? It would appear that they were too costly.

10

In addition to lamps, and preceding them, there were various wood-burning devices, torches, torch-candles and later candles of a modern type. Candles are commonly thought to be older than lamps but this is not a fact. In translations various devices have been called candles for lack of a better word, but biblical scholars inform us that there is no word in the Scriptures that can be accurately translated "candle." What little description we have of the various candle-like devices used by the Romans indicates that they were more like little torches. It is impossible to say just when a torch becomes a candle but there is one test. The purpose of the fat or resin on a torch is to help the large wick to burn; the purpose of the wick in a true candle is to draw up the melted tallow so it can be burned. A candle is almost all tallow and a torch almost all wick.

Simple Lamps

Simple lamps are lamps that have no loose or removable parts. They are, so to speak, all in one piece except for suspension hooks, etc. This group includes pan lamps, crusies and other types of grease lamps; also wick-support lamps or Betties and float lamps. The latter are an exception to the general rule for they have a simple wick holder, but as a type they are very old.

Float Lamps

These lamps are so named because their wicks are either floated on the surface of the oil by some buoyant device or supported there by wires. We know they are at least 5000 years old, for a handsome float lamp was found in the tomb of King Tut-Ankh-Amen. This is evidently not typical of the lamps used by the common people but these are mentioned by Herodotus, who lived in the fifth century B. C. He described them as saucers or bowls with floating wicks. The famous "eternal light" which hung in the Erechtheum in Athens in the fourth century B.C. must have been a float lamp inasmuch as no other type of lamp could have held enough oil to last for an entire year. It may have had a cotton wick (Pausanius I. 26-7) but this "perpetual lamp" which intrigued Middle Age scholars (Licetus, *De Lucernis Antiquorum*, 1621) could hardly have burned for a year without some attention.

The oldest pictures of float lamps are found in early Christian miniatures—some as old as the seventh century A.D. These have the appearance of large ornate pierced lanterns and it is assumed that they were illuminated by float lamps because no other type would be suitable. The oldest picture of float lamps is a detail in a tenth century miniature. This shows a small wheel-type chandelier with seven float lamps, shaped like wine glasses with the feet broken off. There are still chandeliers of this type in German castles and cathedrals, including the huge one at Hildesheim. Sketches made thirty years ago show similar lamps still in their sockets. A later picture of a float lamp—of rather impractical shape—is by Martin Schongauer who died in 1491 (See Plate 25). It is one of a series depicting both the wise and the foolish virgins. It is not quite clear why the artist chose such large lamps for the virgins to carry at the wedding. With lamps as large as this there would have been no lack of oil, even though part of the lamp was filled with water. Possibly there was a religious association, Schongauer having seen float lamps in the cathedrals, or he may have chosen a large lamp to make it conspicuous. Either way we are fortunate to have these

12

charming and instructive engravings. (Biblical scholars say that the virgins probably carried torches.)

John Stow's *Survey of London* was published in 1598, unfortunately without any pictures, but he has this to say about lamps: "On feast days every man's door was shadowed with green birch, long fennel and orpin......(and there were) ......lamps of glass with oil in them burning all night." This is the first descriptive reference to Christmas lights, as we now call them. We can be reasonably sure that they were float lamps because any other type of lamp would not stay lighted outdoors in the wind. We can assume that they were blown glass lamps, which might have been cheerfully colored, but they were not the thick pressed-glass kind of lamp with diamond or knobby patterns sought for by collectors today, as pressed glass was not known at that time.

There was one eighteenth-century American who knew at least a little about almost everything—Benjamin Franklin. He describes a float lamp that he made himself while sailing for England via Madeira in 1762.

"During the passage to Madeira, the weather being warm and the cabin windows open for the air, the candles at night flared and run very much. At Madeira we got oil and with a common glass tumbler slung in wire and suspended from the ceiling and a little wire hoop for the wick furnished with corks to float it on the oil, I made an Italian lamp. The glass at the bottom contained water to about one third of its depth; another third was taken up by the oil; the other third was left empty that the sides of the glass might protect the flame from the wind......The lamp was kept burning all night as a watch-light, till the oil was spent and only water remained."

Night lights or floating tapers were used in great quantities in Europe during the nineteenth century and presumably before. To quote from Hough's Bulletin No. 141, p. 52:

"Night lights as they are commonly called, consist of a disc of cork, wood or paper in the center of which a short bit of taper (wax impregnated candle wick) is fixed. This floats on the oil or is buoyed up by a triangular or cross-shaped piece of metal, the points of which are tipped with cork. Nuremburg was a center from which enormous quantities were distributed......A box of these has been received (in the museum) from Philadelphia where they were said to have been used in 1820."

A reference to the use of night lights in the United States is found in Miss Leslie's *House Book* published in New York in 1848:

"To burn all night in a chamber no lights are so cheap and so convenient as floating tapers. When travelling put a small box of these in your trunk. At night ask for an old teacup full of oil, on top of which you place the float with the wick in it. In the morning take the float out of the cup with the little tweezers that come with it. The best floating tapers are those with wooden floats. They come in boxes from London containing a float, a pair of tweezers and tapers enough to burn every night for months; the cost is but 25 cents."

Old float lamps are rare. It is reported that they are still used in the West Indies and wicks with floats for use in churches can be purchased today in the North End of

14

Boston. A float lamp is such a simple affair that it cannot be readily identified if the float is missing—and it always is. The only one known to the author is in the Harrison Gray Otis House Museum in Boston. This has survived because it has an attractive lithophane screen. The glass font is cylindrical, flaring abruptly at the top. There are other specimens, believed by their owners to be float lamps —and perhaps they are. Any glass container with straight or slightly flaring sides might be a float lamp. If it has a peg or stem an inch or more long and three-quarters of an inch in diameter and especially if it shows signs of age, it could be a float lamp from a chandelier or some similar fixture. Pictures of float lamps are also rare. The few that have been found are shown in Plates 25, 26 and 27.

Fig 1. A 13th century float lamp

Grease Lamps

Pan Lamps, Crusies and Wick-Support Lamps

Lamps seem to have developed from two geographical centers: oil-burning lamps from Egypt, the Near East and the Mediterranean countries; grease lamps from Central Europe. The first center had olive oil. The second had none and was forced to use animal fat. Since inhabitants of these more northerly countries depended on their flocks and herds for food, there was an abundance of it. The clay lamps of the Romans are not adapted to burn this. Clay is not a good conductor of heat and grease lamps depend on both the direct heat from the flame and the heat absorbed by the lamp itself to liquefy the fat around the wick. Although the Romans did have bronze lamps they were too costly for common use. Due to these and possibly other causes and conditions, the use of clay lamps was limited to countries where the olive tree flourishes, while simple iron grease lamps developed in the more northerly countries.

These iron grease lamps were pan lamps and crusies, which are easy to cast or forge because they are shallow. Prehistoric man in Great Britain cast bronze axes. By the eighth century, the art of the smith-armorer was so well advanced that forged iron pan lamps and crusies could easily have been made by the village smith. Such lamps must have been fairly common during the Middle Ages and later. There may be a few of them still in existence, but it is almost impossible to date them, since lamps used in Middle Europe in the eighth century differ so little from those of the seventeenth century, so far as we know.

The shallow, flat lamps that have been used from the beginning are now called grease lamps when they are made of metal. The oldest known lamp, the caveman's stone lamp, is technically a grease lamp and in fact grease was what was burned in it. The specimen illustrated in Plate 21 is so well made, so carefully proportioned and decorated, that it is evident there were rougher lamps much earlier. The chalk lamps found in prehistoric English mines are deeper because chalk is much easier to work than sandstone. Other primitive races such as the Hawaiians and the Eskimos have used similar but much larger lamps.

Any lamp whose wick rests on the bottom, not overhanging or resting against the edge, is commonly called a "pan lamp," or sometimes a " saucer lamp. " Such lamps have been used from prehistoric times down to the present since this is the simplest possible form of a lamp. For instance, in an emergency, a Victorian housewife could improvise a lamp from a saucer half full of melted fat, with a twist of cloth for a wick. Early metal containers are so simple that nothing distinguishes them as lamps. If any of them have survived, there is nothing to identify them. Those that we are able to identify are more complex, such as the sixteenth-century cast iron specimens in the Dreyfus Collection, now in Old Sturbridge Village in Massachusetts.

Pan Lamps in the Dreyfus Collection
(From *The Rushlight*)

The Dreyfus Collection of lighting devices was assembled many years ago by M. Emile Dreyfus, an art dealer of Geneva, Switzerland. It is now on display in Old Sturbridge,

Massachusetts. These lamps range from a prehistoric stone lamp to a variety of mechanized lamps of the early nineteenth century. There are over a hundred pan lamps showing every possible variation in shape and design. Two of them bear dates in the late seventeenth century, so that with the principles of period design and analogous forms in other kinds of iron work to assist, it will be possible to build up a plausible theory concerning these little known devices. One of them still contains a wick and some of a waxy substance last burned in it, which may not be typical of what was burned in it originally. (See Plate 4, Nos. 18, 22, 58 and the two at the left; also Plate 5.)

A few lamps are exceptional in that they have wick supports. This illustrates the crossing of influences in the development of lighting which makes tracing its course so difficult. Light on the origin of the pan lamp is thrown by one of this type in the collection. It is a bronze lamp, rectangular in form and about four by six inches. Its depth is about that of a conventional pan lamp half an inch or less. It has a handle and four very short feet or rests. The rim or edges are nicely moulded but a part of the front end has unfortunately been broken off, so that it is impossible to tell if there was originally a lip for the wick. The general character of the remaining shape, however, would indicate that there was none. Therefore it would be considered a pan lamp and not a shallow grease lamp or crusie.

The large number of pan lamps in the Dreyfus and Von Benesch collections indicate that they were far more common in the Alpine countries than were wick channel types like the Betty. Pan lamps have the advantage that they do not drip seriously because the wick rests on the bottom instead of overhanging the edge. For this and other reasons, which we can only surmise, pan lamps seem to have been popular in Central Europe at the same time that crusies and wick support lamps were popular in Scotland and in other countries bordering the North Sea.

Wick Channel Lamps or Crusies

As indicated earlier, the crusie or wick channel lamp should be distinguished from the pan lamp; the general term "grease lamp" is too broad for adequate identification of either form.

Morever, certain Continental lamps that have grease containers similar to the crusie are not properly "crusies." The Betty lamp, although it will burn hard fats satisfactorily, is a much better lamp than other grease lamps, and is commonly designated as the "Betty."

A crusie is a deep pan lamp *with a channel for the wick*. They are found in many shapes, round and square, but a typical crusie is pear-shaped and about an inch deep. Usually they are made of wrought iron. They are apt to have a half bail for suspension, since their round bottoms are not suited for table use unless they have legs—which few of them do. Although cast brass wick channel lamps from the Mediterranean area may have flat bottoms, they are usually designed for suspension as well; in the only sixteenth century pictures we have of these lamps, they are suspended from the ceiling.

The first lamps of the wick channel type were the old clay lamps with a pinched-up edge for the wick (Plate 4–83). The northern type is a wrought iron adaptation of this clay model. Simple clay lamps may have been copied by the Romans in the early days of the Republic, but their later lamps were covered and had a hole for the wick. However, it is not in Italy but in the countries to the northward that we find typical crusies.

19

All grease lamps except Betties are very untidy. The melted fat around the wick, at the hot end of the lamp, runs down the outside and drips from the bottom. Southern cast brass wick-slot lamps sometimes have a small drip catcher. Northern crusies may have a drip catcher of the same shape as the font but occasionally one is found with a pear-shaped font and a round or even square drip pan. Lamps with both pans alike have been whimsically called "Phoebe" lamps but the more descriptive term "double crusie" is to be preferred.

Once a grease lamp is lighted—which is not always easy— the heat from the flame melts the fat around the wick, but the fat farther away needs to be pushed toward the flame occasionally. One improvement on the simple crusie is a device to tip the pan in order to help the flow of fuel toward the front. (See Plates Nos. 28 and 29.) Saw teeth are cut in the half bail and as the fat is consumed the pan can be tipped by setting it forward a notch.

Crusies rarely have legs but there are a few so equipped as shown at the top of Plate 30.

It is almost impossible to determine where a given wrought-iron crusie was made or in what century. In the United States National Museum there is one old specimen that is definitely dated as a fourteenth-century piece. There is another which came from Dedham, Massachusetts. To the casual observer, one is as old as the other. And within the past fifteen years, a copper double crusie was purchased in Sweden, where they were being made for the Laplanders. Nevertheless, it is possible that a given specimen with the marks of age on it is a sixteenth-century piece, although the chances are greatly against it, for the older such utensils are, the less is the chance that they will have survived.

The word "crusie" is not to be found in the Oxford Dictionary; "cruse" is defined as an oil container and the word was so used by the translators of the St. James version of the Bible. "Crusie", however, is an accepted Scotch term and the lamp itself is described by James Barrie in *Auld Licht Idylls* but with slightly different spelling.

> "The cruizey was all the light Thrums had in those days although it is only to be seen now in a few old houses in the glens...It is shaped like the palm contracted and deepened to hold liquid. Whale oil was used and the wick was a rush which was sold by herd's boys at a halfpenny the bundle. This iron (lamp) was placed in another slightly larger one but of the same shape, for in time the oil dripped over the upper lamp. The whole was then hung by a cleek or hook close to the person using it."

In the Channel Islands the crusie was called a "crasset" as the following excerpts from an article in the *Guernsey Star* (1908) indicate. According to this a crasset is an open pan lamp with a wick channel and a curved half bail attached to a suspension hook—in short, a crusie.

> "The crasset probably stems from ancient pottery vessels—and since our 18th-century poet Metivier mentions clay crassets, we may take it that they were once used here. They were fragile and when the longer-lived iron lamps were available, they were thrown out. Some old people continued to use them until twenty-five years ago, but difficulty in obtaining the kind of oil formerly used, eventually put an end to their use."

Crusies are usually one-piece utensils, but occasionally one sees a rare specimen with a cover and the rarest of all, one on a vertical standard, is shown in Plate 31.

21

A crusie with a cover not only gives the lamp a finished appearance but the space left for the wick acts as a rudimentary wick tube and limits the size of the flame. There are also cast brass types that are forms of multiple-font wick-channel lamps. These, as a type, are very old. They are all intended to be hung from the ceiling or from an arm projecting from the wall. One of these was dug up in England some years ago. In general appearance it was like Besson's lamp shown in Plate 24. Local antiquarians thought it was brought to Britain during the Roman occupation. Even if it is not as old as the second century, it is certainly of early medieval origin. A similar lamp is shown as a detail in Rembrandt's " Christ Driving the Money Changers from the Temple" and there is a fine specimen in the Gardner Museum in Boston. This is a synagogue or sabbath lamp, good specimens of which are often seen in the shops, but are not likely to be very old.

Witch Lamps

These heavy cast iron utensils are technically wick channel lamps (Plate 30). We do not know how old they are or what they burned—grease or whale oil. It is hard to believe that suet or tallow could have been burned in them satisfactorily because they are so much deeper than other grease lamps. By tradition, they are supposed to have shed what little light there was in the Salem gaol where those accused of witchcraft were confined. This popular name for these lamps has no factual or circumstantial background. In fact there is evidence that some of them are nineteenth-century pieces. However, it has never been proven that witch lamps were not used in jails and we may as well accept the name.

A heavy, thick cast-iron lamp of this type has certain advantages, or could have. If it were well heated in front of the fire, grease would be liquefied and the mass of the lamp, combined with the heat from the flame, would tend to keep it warm for some time. But we will never know how our seventeenth-century ancestors managed their lamps.

The late Charles Ayres, a railroad shop superintendent, once said that these lamps were made for machine shop use as late as 1870. There may well have been some specific purpose or particular use for which "witch lamps" were well adapted, so well in fact that they continued in use from the seventeenth to the nineteenth centuries, in New England. Whatever their use here, they originated in England, where a rusted specimen has recently been dug up. This, however, is not necessarily very old. It might have been buried less than a century ago. For a more modern specimen, see plate 30.

Pottery Lamps
(From *The Rushlight*)

No one knows where the first pottery lamps were used. It is thought that they had their source in Egypt. If so, they were undoubtedly float lamps of vase shape. Alabaster forms of the kind found in tombs seem to have been intended for that purpose. Except for a few paintings in tombs, which suggest float lamps but give no information as to their material, there seems to be little documentary evidence. If early simple bowl-shaped lamps were used in Egypt, none remains that can be recognized as a lighting device.

(Discussion of classical lamps in the article has been omitted here.)

23

During the Roman occupation of Britain, some lamps of distinctive type were made in potteries there or brought into the country by traders. They are described in William Chaffers' *Pottery and Porcelain.* Chaffers says the lamps found in England are seldom of bronze but of terra cotta. Specimens excavated in London are rounded in form with blunt beaks but without handles (Plate 32, figure 5). These lamps are almost always undecorated and, in fact, are of crude character. When in use they were placed upon flat earthenware trays...One example has a hole through the center for placing it on a pointed holder. It has a black glaze, ornamented with red bands. It, too, was found in London. Another, excavated on a pottery site in Colchester, has, over the body of the lamp, a curious hood-shaped contrivance of questionable function, for it could not have shielded the flame in the projecting spout (Plate 32, figure 6).

With the fall of the Roman Empire, Europe reverted to primitive pottery devices that revived or perpetuated crude types, and no advance was made during the Middle Ages. In the Mohammedan countries the lamps of shell-like form, the beaked lamp with a conical filler and other more simple lights were the common types. It is probable that pottery bowls or saucers were generally used as float lamps during the medieval period. Even in Saxon England the plain open lamp was known and several examples have been excavated in recent years. One found in Yorkshire had a handle and was supported by a stem. There is also a "cresset" or large bowl of the twelfth century preserved in the Lancaster Museum. Examples of medieval pottery are, however, rare, as they were used for a number of purposes and easily broken.

It is certain that no mechanical improvement over the lamps mentioned occurred during the Middle Ages. Each area of civilization continued to employ the devices that had come down to it from ancient times. Occasionally lamp types were carried from one part of the world to another by seafaring men or colonists, but with all their differences, they retained essentially the same primitive character until the end of the eighteenth century. Only with the rise of science in modern times were better lamps invented. Hough (*Fire as an Agent in Human Culture*) finds no characteristic types in England, Scotland or northern Europe. " The lamps of the Italian folk are mostly glazed and decorated majolica and often excellent specimens of the art. These lamps do not follow the classical traditions but are North African in origin." Of Spanish pottery lamps Hough says that George Borrow saw at San Lucas in 1838 " a small earthen pan filled with water and oil, on which floated a small piece of card with a lighted wick in the middle, called a ' mariposa.' " He also notes : " Moorish lamps encountered in Spain are of terracotta, glazed or unglazed, or of bronze."

(The discussion of pottery lamps in the Middle and Far East has been omitted here).

In America, the only aborigines who possessed a lamp were the Eskimos. We are all familiar with their large stone lamps and heaters but perhaps less so with a type of pottery lamp found among them. It is a deep saucer shaped of clay by hand and dark brown in color. It is thought that it was introduced to this continent from Asia. Pottery lamps were brought to this hemisphere by Spanish settlers and were used in Spanish America for centuries. No other colonists brought pottery lamps to America or made them here, until the Pennsylvania Germans arrived in the eighteenth century.......

A survey of all the published examples of American pottery lamps has been made. There are less than fifteen. One might jump to the conclusion that lamps so rare were made only occasionally. But they were rather common in their day. They almost always appear in the area of German settlement, principally among the so-called Pennsylvania Dutch in that state and in Ohio, among the Moravians in North Carolina, and to some extent at a late period in Tennessee. It is a curious fact, however, that the few examples attributed to particular potters were made by men with English names. These lamps were turned out by country potters who used the local clay. The greater number are of red earthenware, a few of stoneware. With two exceptions, all of the specimens noted have been stand lamps with a base and a handle or handles. Most of them have reservoirs with a lip for a wick rest; three different types have spouts; two have wick supports.

Judging by the probabilities alone, the German settlers would have made the style of lamp familiar to them in their homeland. That they did do this we know, as similar lamps were used by the peasants in northwestern Europe, in Hungary and in Sweden. In Robins (*Story of the Lamp*) Plate XXXIa, three Hungarian specimens are shown which might easily be mistaken for Pennsylvania products. Continental lamps differ in the respect that they usually have a pouring lip in the saucer base. They do, nevertheless, show the ancestry of our American pottery.

In the Smithsonian Institution there is a lamp obtained in Morgantown, West Virginia from a man whose family had worked in a pottery there. This was started shortly after the Revolution by one Foulke, who has been variously supposed to be German, French or English. After 1800 the pottery was run by the Thompson family. The lamp, of red earthenware, with a pinkish red glaze, was made probably before 1840. Dr. Hough says it was "used on the frontier in Virginia and was of English ancestry." He does not mean that the lamp was English, but that it was a descendant of the English pottery lamp known as a

Cornish " chill." Specimens of this same type appear in the Penzance and Truro Museums in Cornwall. One is described as having a red-brown glaze, being eight inches in height, with a four-inch reservoir; the other is shorter, with a greenish-brown glaze, and has the feature of a spout in the base, as in Hungarian and Swedish lamps. There is evidently a relationship between the Cornish and Continental types, which without doubt are the originals of the lamps made in America.

This squatty type of hand lamp (shown in outline in Plate 32, figure 15) was also made in Tennessee of stoneware clay. A lamp in the Bucks Country Museum is illustrated in *Light and Fire Making* by H.C. Mercer, who says of it: " From the boat-shaped earthen lamps of ancient Rome, and from the green majolica ones of candlestick shape used by the Moors today, to a boat-shaped stoneware lamp set upon a stemmed dish filled with 'possum or 'coon fat, as used by a Tennessee moonshiner, there is no change of character. J.T. Goodwin baked one for me of blue clay in 1895." In this instance we have a lamp by a known maker but such are rare. A similar pair of Tennessee lamps, from this or perhaps another pottery, are known to have been made and used in that backward area as late as 1905. All these have reservoirs with lips. Another lamp in this style (Plate 32, figure 16) is of redware. Its marks indicate a period between 1825 and 1854.

Of similar form but far more colorful (Figure 17) is a North Carolina type made by Moravian potters of German descent. The Moravians practiced their craft in Bathabara as early as 1756. The body of this pottery is a light red, decorated with black, green and cream slips on a yellow-brown ground. Some of these lamps have reservoirs of globular form, slightly closed in at the top and with chunky projecting spouts to serve as wick channels (Figure 18).

27

Only two lamps with true spouts have been found, both from Pennsylvania and both perhaps unique in some detail. Another spouted lamp (Figure 20) illustrated by Hayward (*Colonia Lighting*) could hardly have been a type but rather the creation of some individualistic potter. With its cover and curved spout, it resembles a teapot.

In the Landis Valley Museum is a stand lamp (Figure 21) of red pottery nearly eight inches tall that has some peculiar features. Its reservoir is a shallow bowl fitted inside with a wick support in the form of a hollow pottery tube. There is a pottery Betty from Pennsylvania in the Watkins collection, a wheel-turned piece made of redware, having a wick support in the shape of a gutter or half-tube, and provided with a hole at the back for a suspension wire or string.

An article which appeared in *Antiques* for May, 1940, illustrated eight lamps from Pennsylvania, all somewhat different from the specimens described above. Two are real spout lamps, while three others are Betty types with wick supports. This article should be consulted by those wishing further data on this subject (*Early Pottery Lighting Devices in Pennsylvania* by William J. Truax).

Spout Lamps (Oil Burning)

Spout lamps which have the wick *enclosed in a tube* are quite old, as clay lamps from the Near East indicate. One of Hogarth's engravings in the *Rake's Progress* series illustrates their use in the seventeenth century as street lights. If our supply of kerosene were cut off and a heavier, thicker oil were used in its place, the warning lights now used by contractors would have to be replaced by spout lamps. They have always been a favorite for outdoor use. Such lamps have large wicks and are not easily extinguished by the wind; and the font can be made large enough to hold a liberal supply of oil.

Other spout lamps can be divided into two groups: lucernas and Flemish types (Plates 13 and 17 upper row) are for domestic use, while those of the Cape Cod pattern (Plate 16, upper right) are designed for use on wharves and ships and in shops. Many of these lamps are made of tin but others (Plate 3), probably from the Scandinavian countries, are more substantially made of copper. Tall Flemish types are made of sheet brass and lucernas of cast brass. There are other names for spout lamps in addition to those mentioned above, such as mill lamps, pastors' or rabbis' lamps, kyals and others. The number and variety of these names suggest that they have been widely used over a long period of time.

Lucernas

Lamps of the lucerna type but without the standard are quite old. Technically they are similar to earlier clay and bronze spout lamps but with more spouts for additional light. The addition of a standard to permit vertical adjustment was an improvement over the older suspension types. Hough (Bulletin 141) says: "They are an old type that has survived into modern times. They have been treasured both for their artistry and as curios." They may still find a limited use where olive oil is the cheapest illuminant available. Lucernas are made of well-finished cast brass and usually have three or four spouts; one with two or five spouts would be a rarity. One described by Hough as the oldest lucerna in the Smithsonian collection "has on the handle three Roman eagles; mice feed on the oil in the font, while three of the geese that saved Rome from a surprise attack decorate the base." Hough says this is an ancient lamp but he does not estimate its age. Lucernas are rather common in antique shops. They show no signs of age or use and are fully equipped with the easily lost pickwicks and snuffers—sometimes extinguishers as well—and it may be assumed that when they were brought into this country, it was not as duty-free antiques.

There is a type or variant of the old spout lamps, with an added detail of a small drip cup around the wick tube as in lucernas, that is variously called a pastors' or a rabbis' lamp. One of these is shown in Plate 33. Other spout lamps having no particular name are illustrated in Plate 6, nos. 2, 8, 24, and others have the familar-shaped spouts but with tall cylindrical fonts. The glass lamps numbered 4, 25, 78 and 97 in Plate 6 are probably from Bohemia. There is one like No. 78 in the Essex Institute in Salem. These odd-shaped lamps are something of a mystery. They could be all-glass adaptations of the metal Cardan lamps but there seems to be no convenient way of filling them, other than through the wick tube and there is no provision for a burner. One of these lamps, in the Daniels collection, is blackened around the wick hole, which suggests that no removable burner was used. This might be possible if the lamps were well annealed and warmed before lighting—altogether too many "ifs" and "mights".

Flemish Spout Lamps

Flemish-type spout lamps (Plate 13) are fairly common and have apparently been used in the Low Countries from the eighteenth to the late nineteenth centuries, but not further east. Scandinavian patterns (Plate 3) are technically similar but they differ in appearance, being made for outdoor and shop use. Flemish lamps are commonly made of sheet brass and are from eight to twenty-four inches tall, with a conical sand-weighted base flattened on one side to permit the lamp to rest more firmly against the wall when it is suspended by the tab. The font usually sets in a cylindrical holder to which the drip catcher is attached. This holder is often embellished with shallow embossed designs or decorated with punch marks.

Cape Cod Lamps

Cape Cod lamps (Plate 16, top shelf) are the American version of the Scandinavian spout models. Hough says that on the Cape they are called "kyals;" this, however, is not the name by which they are commonly known today. Both the name and the lamps themselves must have come from eastern Europe around the North Sea.

There seems to be no distinctive English model of this lamp but they have evidently been widely used there. In Birmingham they were called "mill" lamps; in Wales, "duck" lamps, doubtless a local version of "Dutch" lamps. They were also called "snotty nose" lamps since they dripped so freely. These lamps may not have had the large drip catcher which the Flemish and Scandinavian types have. Characteristically, the wick tubes and font are set down into a cylinder as deep as the font. This lower portion carries the drip catchers and there is ample room for the drip. These lamps usually have a bail to carry them by and two spouts. Rarely one is found with a single spout and a " D " handle.

It might be noted at this point that the older type of mine lamps were a form of small spout lamps.

Betty and Other Wick-Support Lamps

Most lamp collectors know a Betty lamp when they see one but they might not be able to describe one accurately and fully. The unobtrusive feature that makes it a better lamp than any so far described is a half-round wick support attached to the bottom of the lamp, not touching the sides. In addition to this, a typical Betty has a cover integral with the lamp and a half bail curving up over the top to hold or hang it up by. Most Betties are roughly triangular as crusies are. They may be pear-shaped or a modified cloverleaf pattern, but a round or a square lamp with the above features would still be a Betty—and a rare one too. Of course there are the usual exceptions and borderline cases. Other lamps with wick supports that are not Betties often have names of their own.

If you want a lamp for emergencies following floods and hurricanes, a Betty is a good lamp to have. It will burn mineral oil, salad oil, Crisco, vaseline, and candle ends. A roll of cloth or the cotton from a bottle of pills will do for a wick. It should be started with liquid fuel and once you have the wick properly adjusted you will have as good a light as your eighteenth-century ancestors had. Melted fat or oil will not creep over the edge of the lamp, for any drip from the wick runs back into the font. For these reasons the Betty lamp—under whatever name—has been a popular house lamp from the later part of the Middle Ages in continental Europe to 1850 in the United States. They were used in Spain and probably elsewhere long after that. Betties were the first really satisfactory lamps housewives had.

The origin and derivation of the term "Betty" as the name of a common type of wick-support lamp has been the subject of many discussions. It is indeed a frivolous name for such a sturdy utensil but it has been in use for fifty years or more in New England and is now an accepted term among collectors and dealers. It has been variously claimed that it is a variant of the French *petit, butto* from the isle of Aran, and *besser* from the German and Dutch. Another well-argued derivation is that it comes from the old English word *bete,* meaning "to advantage" and later "to kindle a fire." The writer's choice is *besser* but we could all be wrong. *Besser* means "better" and from this "Betty." The Pilgrims lived in Holland ten years before they came to Plymouth and this would be a very small change to have been made in two centuries. In the seventeenth century, arts and conveniences were more advanced on the continent than they were in England and a Betty lamp may well have been a better lamp than they had at home. There is one in Plymouth, said to have come over in the Mayflower, and another in the New York Museum of Science and Industry that by family tradition was brought to Dorchester, Massachusetts in 1630. The name has evidently been used in Massachusetts for a century or more but there were other names for it in other parts of the country. In the earliest accession records of the United States National Museum, they are called—presumably by the donors—*kays, judies* and *frog* lamps.

We do not know how old Betties or other wick-support lamps are. They are probably older than is commonly supposed. Hough in commenting on one of them in the National Museum says: "This old Italian lamp is a good example of an early device—the wick is supported on a small metal channel soldered to the bottom of the lamp, which obviates the use of a separate drip catcher. The date of this improvement is unknown." What may be the oldest picture of a Betty lamp is shown as a detail in an engraving of a sixteenth century pope's kitchen (Plates 34 and 35). This is from a book published by Bartolomeo Scappi, personal cook for Pope Pius the Fifth. In detailed pictures of two kitchens there are three lamps and a tall flambeau holder. Two lamps are suspended from the ceiling and another over the sink. The details are none too clear but the position of the wicks and the flame indicate that these are not wick channel lamps; the flame does not issue from the very edge of the lamp as it does in older lamps lacking a wick support. In the sixteenth century the arts were more advanced in Italy than they were in England or in Central Europe. Cardan's lamp was invented in this century and in the same country. If there were to be improvements in lamps, Italian artisans were most likely to provide them. The sketch of Cardan's lamp shown in Plate 24 strongly suggests that it had either a wick support or a tube. He does not mention this as anything new, so we may conclude that wick supports are as old as 1550 and probably much older.

No one knows how old a given Betty lamp is unless it happens to be a very rare one like the one shown in Plate 40 with inscribed date. But its form and the material of which it is made should give us a few clues. The older lamps are made either of hand-forged and formed iron or of cast iron. The font is all in one piece except for the cover and the wick support. Seventeenth century French guild regulations provided that "No copper lamps shall be soldered but shall be made in one piece, nor shall any old lamps be repaired and sold as new" (Boileau, *Le Livre des Metiers*). Such copper lamps might antedate iron lamps, since copper can be worked cold by frequent annealing, but we never see any of them. They have long since been thrown into the melting pot. Lamps of any material, if soldered or brazed where the sides join the bottom, are likely to be eighteenth or nineteenth century pieces. Tin Betties were made as late as 1850. Lamps that are beaten out or are made of cast iron are likely to have sides curving outward from the bottom since this construction is easier for both the iron worker and the foundryman.

Signed or marked pieces of silver or pewter are always eagerly sought and marked Betties are no exception. At a meeting of the Rushlight Club over fifty such lamps were exhibited. The following makers were identified: John Lang; P. D. (Peter Derr); John Schmitz; J. Eby; J. Post; F. Hurxthal. Both the names and the care given to details are evidence that most of them are of Pennsylvania origin.

The name M & R Boker was also noted on a few lamps but this company was a New York distributor. Some of these lamps bore serial numbers and their construction suggested that they might have been made in a press of some sort. One was dated 1850. There is often something that will identify the maker even if his name or initials are lacking—the shape of the font, the style of the suspension chain and the twists and ornaments on hook and bail. The knob on the cover may be strictly functional or it may be a bird or some emblem. Some have punch-marked decorations on the cover. All of these are the work of the Pennsylvania Germans, who so slowly relinquished their old world customs and artistry. It should be mentioned, however, that the initials on a lamp may be those of the owner and not the maker.

Pewter Betty Lamps

Betties made of sheet brass or copper are rare, possibly more so than those made of pewter, but the latter are more industriously sought after. Twenty years ago a leading collector claimed with good reason that there could be no such thing as a pewter Betty lamp because the melting point of pewter is so low that it will melt in a candle flame; even if the wick support were made of tin, the flame would be so close to the body of the lamp that its nose would be melted off. But as often happens, it was not long before someone appeared with a pewter Betty to confound the experts. Since then others have been found, but not many. They are very rare. This being so, no one who is fortunate enough to own one is going to put oil and a wick in it and risk his lamp for the benefit of either school of thought. So we do not know whether pewter Betty lamps are practical or not. It has been suggested that they were not intended to be, that they are apprentices' practice pieces, curious but impractical utensils. They are certainly curious, particularly when we remember that the seventeenth-century meaning of the word was careful or skillful. (See Plates 36, 37 and 38.)

Other Wick-Support Lamps

Not all wick support lamps are Betties. From the Mediterranean countries come cast brass lamps with a wick support, but lacking a cover and the distinctive shape of the more westerly types. There are also tall lamps—usually pewter—such as the one shown in Plate 5, no. 26. This is called a convent lamp. A similar lamp is shown in Plate 11, upper left. See also the rare semi-porcelain lamp in Plate 41.

Kettle Lamps

Kettle lamps have either a wick support or a support with a very short tube at the end. These tall iron lamps with the font swinging on trunnions are of German or German-American origin. The ones commonly seen come from Pennsylvania. They lack decoration or embellishment but the slender support rising from a circular or tripod base is often as well proportioned as a Greek column. The kettle or font is cylindrical, with the depth somewhat greater than the diameter. It would be interesting to know how these were formed. One with a round base is shown in Plate 15, no. 4 and another with four legs is shown in one of the plates of the Rushlight exhibition (Plate 16). A very rare wall type appears twice in Plate 7 (No. 13 and the unnumbered lamp just under it). The ring at the bottom of the latter was doubtless put there for some good purpose but we do not know what it was. Rarely one sees a kettle lamp in brass. They have semi-spherical fonts and are European types—possibly French. Often, in addition to a cover, they have a handle. The font can be tipped to soak the wick (temporarily) in the oil or melted fat and the trunnions return it to a level position. An example is shown in Plates 8 and 13—second shelves. Two other Pennsylvania models are seen in Plate 9—next to top shelf.

Cardan's Lamp (Oil Burning)

There is one lamp that should be mentioned here although it had little effect on the lighting problems of the common people. This is Cardan's lamp of 1550 (Plate 24) which was the best lamp available from that date until the later part

38

of the eighteenth century. It neither gave more light nor distributed it better than a Betty lamp on a standard, but it did have a greatly improved oil font, later adopted by Argand. There are many of these lamps in the Von Benesch Collection (Plate 39), which indicates that the Cardan lamp was popular among the wealthy and possibly those who were willing to try something new.

Jerome Cardan was an Italian doctor of medicine and a physicist. He did not invent the fountain feed that is the best part of his lamp. He probably found a description of it in a manuscript written by one of the Greek engineers, either Heron or Philon, but he was first to reduce their theories to practice. He did invent the universal joint so necessary to all automobile transmissions.

Following is a translation from his *De Subtilitate* (1550) :

"By the urge of a vacuum, water mounts on high (over the edge) of a tub and fills an earthen jar, so emptying the tub. Using this principle a marvelous lamp has been made. It is in the form of a round tower made of tin (or pewter, 'ex stanno') firmly joined (air tight) except for the hole "D", through which the oil is poured until it is full. When it is set upon its base, all the oil will escape through this hole......By what means then when the burning wick at "F" has consumed all the oil (in the canal "E"), shall more oil flow out of the hole "D" into the canal "E"? To explain this, the nature of a vacuum must be found, to discover if the oil is drawn by the heat or descends of its own accord......However, experience shows that the lamp always continues to burn and little by little it is emptied of its oil."

The engraving of a *terb'antier* on page forty-one is the best picture we have of seventeenth-century lighting devices and there were few changes or improvements before the final quarter of the eighteenth century. *Ferblantiers* or tinsmiths were the principal lamp makers of this period, although lamps of iron, brass and copper were made by the blacksmith, brazier and coppersmith. The lighting devices here depicted were doubtless chosen by the artist for their curious interest and their display value, inasmuch as none of the older grease lamps are shown. It is hard to date this picture for there were three generations of Lamessins, all engravers. The one who seems most likely to have cut this plate lived from 1634 to 1694 although the inclusion of a spring type candleholder might suggest a slightly later date. We are fortunate to have this detailed picture.

Among tin utensils shown in this engraving are:
one pricket-type and two socket-type candlesticks
three spout lamps—one with a "peg"
two sconces
two (possibly three) Cardan lamps
two lanterns and the large square one used as a body
three spring-type candlesticks with shades as described
and illustrated in Abbe' Pluch's *Encyclopedie* of 1734
The device on the head which suggests a reflector of some sort has not been identified.

Time or Clock Lamps

Technically, a time lamp is a Cardan lamp with a roughly cylindrical or pear-shaped glass font, to which are attached two or three pewter bands having raised figures to indicate the hour by measuring the oil level. All observed specimens

40

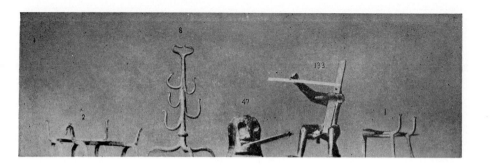

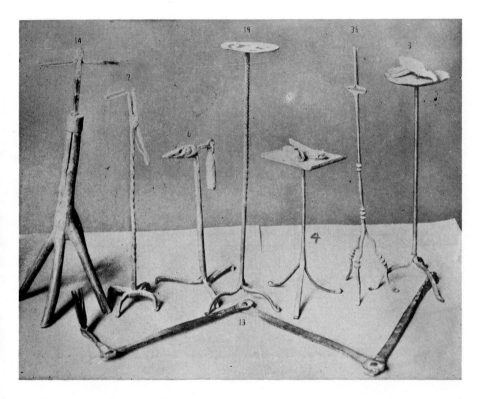

Plate 1 Splintholders and firepans (From *Das Beleuchtungswesen* by Von Benesch) (See page 5)

Note: It is not always feasible to identify each and every lighting device in group pictures. With few exceptions all commonly recognized types have been described and illustrated elsewhere in the book.

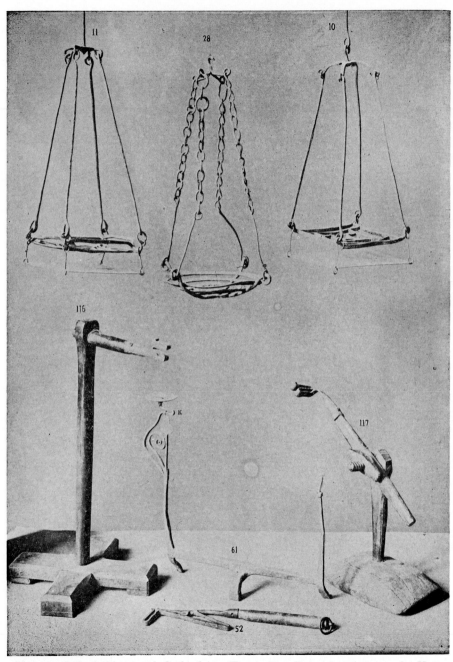

Plate 2 Splintholders and firebaskets (From *Das Beleuchtungswesen* by Von Benesch) (See page 6)

Plate 3   Upper row: Tall wick support lamp; two spout lamps; an Eastern-
type wick channel lamp with drip catcher and a Japanese fixture with two
pan lamps.   *Other lamps are:* two Hanukkahs and a small taper holder;
three whale oil lamps and brass lamps from the Far East   (See pages 29,
31 & 83)

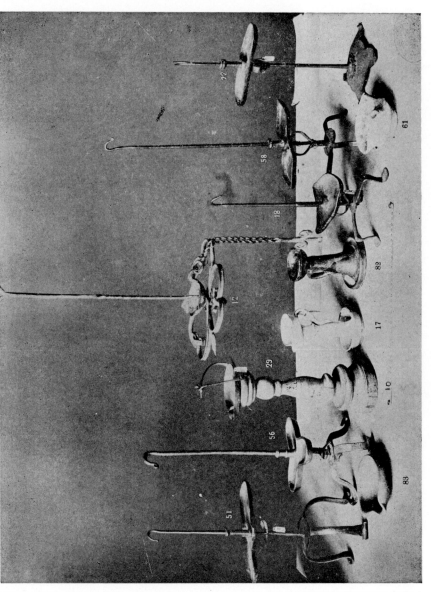

Plate 4 Pan lamps and clay lamps from the Near East (See page 18)

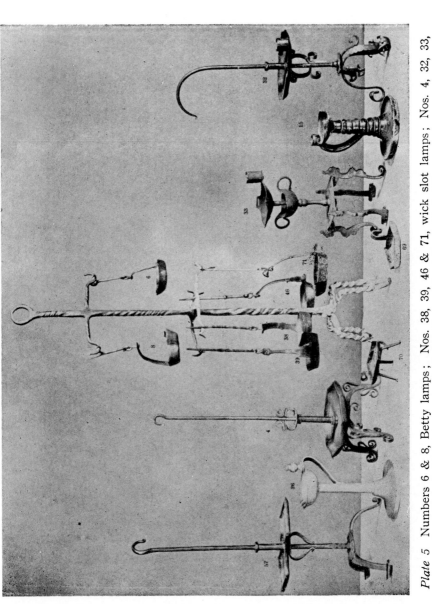

Plate 5 Numbers 6 & 8, Betty lamps; Nos. 38, 39, 46 & 71, wick slot lamps; Nos. 4, 32, 33, 57 & 69, pan lamps, No. 26, pewter convent lamp (See pages 18 & 37)

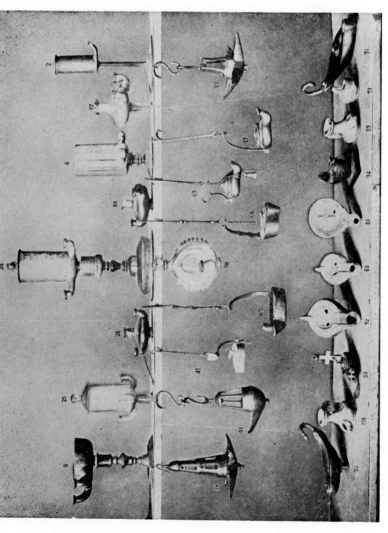

Plate 6 Numbers 2, 4, 8, 24, 25, 26, 66, 69, 97, 98, metal and glass spout lamps; Nos. 47, 67, 68, Betty lamps, the latter has added wick tube; Nos. 86, 91, 92, multiple wick channel lamps, Eastern type; No. 78, a glass Cardan (?) lamp. Other lamps in lower row from the Near East and elsewhere (See page 30)

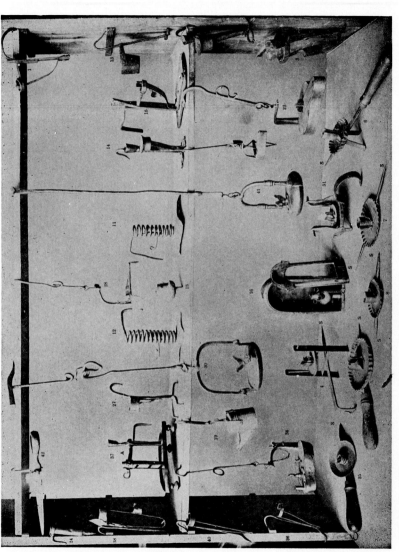

Plate 7 Mine and cellar lights. Number 1 (and others) Alpine type flambeaux or torch holders; "S", sticking tommies; Nos. 23 & 28, Betty lamps, No. 34 is improved; Nos. 19, 30 & 41, miners' lamps; several candleholders, No. 37 has notches for candle lift; Nos 9 & 13, kettle lamps; Nos. 14 & 27 (?) (See pages 38 & 116)

Plate 8 From the Ingraham Collection (See page 38)

Plate 9 From the Ingraham Collection (See pages 7, 38 & 52)

Plate 10 From the Ingraham Collection

Plate 11 From the Ingraham Collection (See pages 37 & 47)

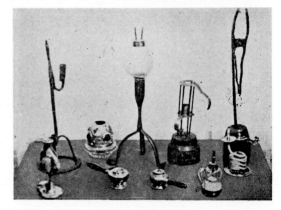

Plate 12 From the Kenneth Mathews Collection

Plate 13 From the Julius and Frances Daniels Collection (See pages 29, 31 & 38) *Upper row:* Two lucernas, two Flemish spout lamps and a Sabbath lamp (*center*). Other specimens include a brass lard oil lamp with button turn-up; two trunnion lamps and a rolling lamp

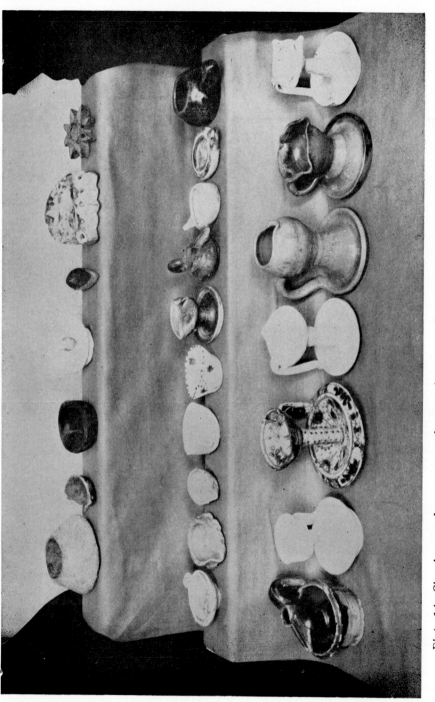

Plate 14 Clay lamps of many types from various countries (Julius and Frances Daniels Collection)

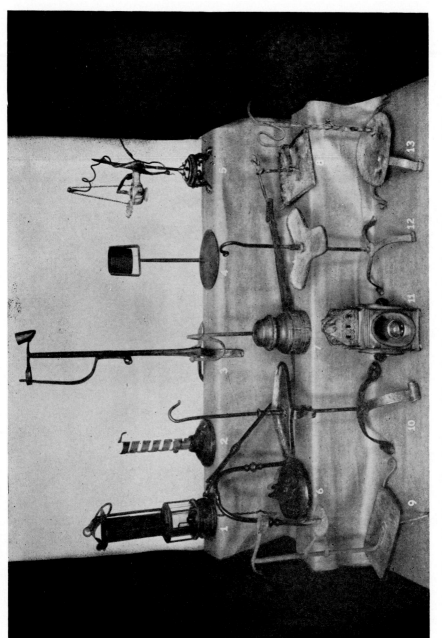

Plate 15 From the Julius and Frances Daniels Collection (See page 38 and Plate 16)

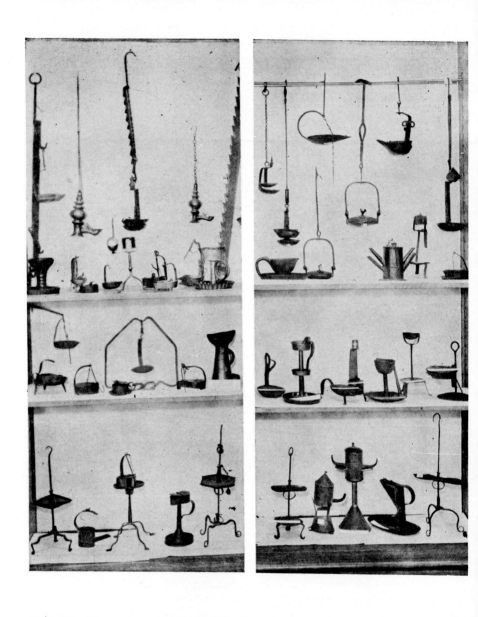

Plate 16 Grease lamps. Rushlight Club Exhibit   (See pages 29, 31 & 38)
Plate 15, previous page, additional data: Nos. 1 and 6, miners' lamps, new
and old style; No. 2, candleholder, spiral type; No. 4, kettle lamp ; No. 5,
bronze lamp on stand; No. 7, rushlight holder; Nos. 8, 10 and 12, pan lamps;
Nos. 9 and 13, candle (?), link or taper holders ; No. 11, bull's eye lantern,
18th c.

Plate 17 Patent lamps. Rushlight Club Exhibit (See pages 29, 63 & 64)

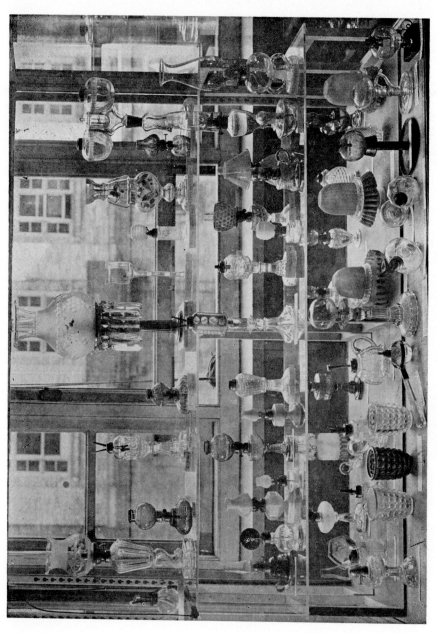

Plate 18 Glass lamps. Rushlight Club Exhibit

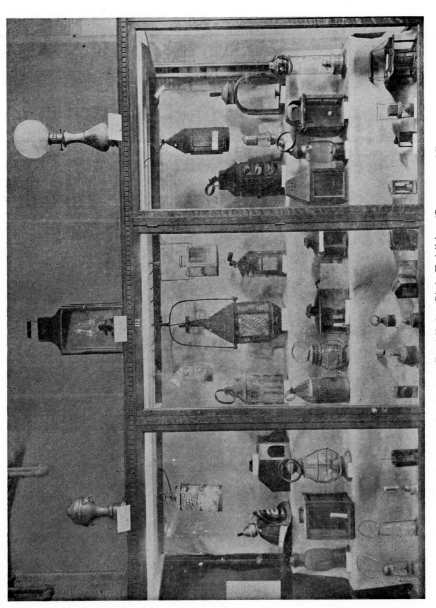

Plate 19 Lanterns. Rushlight Club Exhibit (See page 86)

Plate 20 Kerosene or coal oil lamps (See page 88)

Fig. 2 17th century ferblantier (see page 40)

are made of pewter. See Plate 42. Most of these have raised figures or, rarely, etchings on the font, which cover a period of eight or nine hours, but this varies with individual specimens.

It is hard to believe that these lamps, whenever they were made, were anything but a curious and intriguing specimen of the pewterer's or lampmaker's art. They seem highly impractical as the font on many of them is too small to hold oil enough for eight hours. There is no wick regulator and the height of the flame is critical. They must have been troublesome to fill and particularly to fill to the exact time on the font at which you intend—and must—light the lamp. They are, however, rare and curious and you will be fortunate to find one offered for sale. As a source of light they were as good as any small Cardan lamp. They are found with one, two and even three burners. But the font seems rather small for multiple burners.

Fig. 3 Cardan lamp, 18th century

Lamps With Vertical Wick Tubes

The average seventeenth and eighteenth-century family, when it did not burn splints, rushlights or tallow dips, must have used grease lamps for what little artificial light they had. These flat lamps had various disadvantages. If a soft grease was used, occasionally it had to be pushed up around the wick and the latter scraped or picked up. They dripped melted fat and were generally untidy. If oil was used there was the danger of spilling if the lamp was moved or hit accidentally. In addition these lamps distributed the light very poorly. If they rested directly on a table, all the light went upward; if elevated on a stand or suspended from a beam, the distribution was better but the oil font cast a wide shadow. There must have been a demand for better lamps and by 1750 there were doubtless many metal workers and inventors engaged in this problem. Out of this came lamps with vertical wick tubes. One reason why such lamps had never been commonly available was the lack of a thin oil—an oil thin enough to wet the wick up to the top of wick tubes. There probably were thin oils but they were too expensive for common use: oil pressed from nut meats and possibly the best grades of olive oil. Cheaper oils must have been developed by about 1775. For example, in the *American Museum* for February 1789, a method is given for "edulcorating" whale oil to render it less viscous. Cyrus Eaton in his *Anna s of Warren Maine* (1790) says, "By the close of the century, spermaceti oil

43

lamps made of tin or brass gradually came into use in place of candles." These must have been John Miles patent lamps, which are described later.

Lamps with vertical or nearly vertical wick tubes are probably quite old but their use seems to have been limited. A shallow bronze lamp with a slanting wick tube was excavated in the old marketplace in Athens. Roman lanterns had lamps with vertical wick tubes and a few illustrations of other lamps in European museums show burners with vertical wick tubes but these might have been alcohol lamps. Some kettle lamps and at least one other (Plate 41) have what are substantially the same kind of tubes. There are also priests' lamps to be described later. Some types of classical lamps had a limited sort of wick tube provided by the thickness of the clay or metal around the hole for the wick. This practice could not have been copied extensively during the Middle Ages for but two examples of wick-hole lamps have been noted. One is a tin peg lamp illustrated by D'Allemagne and the other a cast brass lamp with the font on trunnions, said to have come from the ancestral chateau of the Marquis de Lafayette in Avignon (Plate 43). It seems unlikely that this lamp is older than 1750. If it is complete, as its maker intended it to be, it proves that wick-hole lamps were still used in the eighteenth century.

Burners intended to be set over a hole in the top of the font—drop burners—are generally accepted as the first vertical wick tubes to come into common use. It is a reasonable assumption that glass peg lamps were the first to be provided with this new burner. Thorpe in his *History of G ass* illustrates such a lamp and says it is as old as the fourteenth century. It is not shown here as the halftone lacks detail but it is like the round glass peg lamps shown in Plates 26 and 45. These lamps evidently could not have had floating wicks, so they must have had some sort of burner, either a tube in a cork or a drop burner. The lamp shown in Plate 46 is worthy of notice because it has evidence of use still upon it. The font is much older than the rest of the lamp. Note especially the burner with its little tab, as it will be referred to later.

There are two types of drop burners: an all metal type and others to which a cork disc or stopper have been added. Most of the former have a groove around the edge, possibly to locate it on the hole at the top of the lamp or to raise up a fillet on the upper side to catch any excess oil. Others are only saucer-shaped discs, which conceivably could fit into a small depression around the hole in the lamp. Burners with cork bushings are supposed to be an American improvement, as glass lamps with a short neck, instead of a hole, were made for them in this country. Burners with the little tab mentioned above are thought to be of Continental origin but they could have been imitated here. The following comments on cork burners are from an article by Charles L. Woodside in *Antiques* for December 1927 and January of the following year. Nothing better on this subject has ever been written.

It would not be surprising to learn that the whale oil lamp had its origin in a cork stopper......What could be more easily accomplished than to thrust a small tube through the length of such a stopper, to insert a wick in the tube, to fill the bottle with oil and apply a flame?

The first type of burner consisted of a cork stopper placed between two tin discs, the upper one larger in diameter than the lower one, through all of which passed the tin tube for a wick, the whole being securely soldered together. The wick tube had a slot on one side through which the wick could be picked up as it burned

45

away. It was made in two sizes: small, with one wick tube; and large, with two wick tubes placed a little apart. It was fitted into the opening of the oil bowl just as one fits a stopper into a bottle. The upper disc was turned up around the edge to prevent the overflow of the oil in case the wick over fed—that is, drew up the oil faster than it could be burned; and a small hole through the disc and cork allowed such surplus oil to run back into the oil bowl.

In the larger burners, the wick tubes were usually one-quarter of an inch in diameter at the top, a little larger at the bottom, and one and three-quarters inches long. The upper disc was one and one-quarter inches in diameter and the tubes, which extended three-eighths above it, were separated about an eighth of an inch. In both sizes the upper discs were sometimes stamped with the word *Patent* but were devoid of further information. See Plate 49.

Pump Lamps

These once popular lamps are said to have been invented by the Abbe de Perigny in 1748. The earliest examples were made of tin but examples commonly seen are pewter. As their name indicates, these lamps pump oil up to the wick. The font is vase-shaped and contains a small plunger-type pump, which functions when the candle-shaped tube, rising from the top, is pumped up and down. This forces oil up into a small reservoir just below the wick plate. This is an early example of the use of a vertical wick and a drop burner, which was discussed in the preceeding pages. These burners are usually missing but no other type could have been used. What are presumably the latest models even have screw-type burners and flat wicks. However, the older types have an oblong hole at the top which strongly suggests that the drop burners had flat wicks also. We do not know enough about these lamps. If we can judge from the numbers of them in collections and elsewhere, they must have been popular among those who could afford them. This seems to have been in the period from 1750 to 1800 but this estimate is based only on circumstantial evidence. Three of these lamps can be seen on the lower shelf of the corner cupboard in Plate 11.

Benjamin Franklin is commonly credited with being the first to point out and prove that a lamp with two wick tubes gives more light than two lamps with single burners. Until just now there has been no direct or circumstantial evidence of this. D'Allemagne in his *Histoire de la Luminaire* quotes one M. Clays as having said that Franklin was the inventor of the twin-tube burner but diligent search has failed to substantiate this reference, which of course does not prove that D'Allemagne was wrong. Fortunately we have a more direct and more nearly contemporary comment on this question.

Frederic Accum (1739–1838) was a contemporary of Franklin and was interested in lighting problems. His *A Practical Treatise on Gas Light*, London 1815, is a classic in the history of gas lighting. On page forty-four he says: " It has been suggested by Dr. Franklin that the flame of two candles joined, give a much stronger light than both of them separately. "

Books now in progress will include all known letters and publications of Dr. Franklin but they will never find all of them. Some future researcher may find something to prove his invention of a twin-tube burner. In the meantime we should give great weight to Accum's statement since the principle of twin tubes is the same as " joined candles. "

Following the invention of Argand and Miles and the development of gas lighting by Windsor, Clegg and Accum, there was much interest in lamps and lighting. Accum's comment implies that anyone well informed on the subject of lamps and lighting knew of Franklin's suggestion, whether it was originally in a letter—possibly to Accum himself— or spoken in a demonstration using the then newly-invented Rumford photometer.

We now know that Franklin was the first to suggest and probably to demonstrate the advantage of two flames mutually warming each other, the principle on which the twin tubes of the whale oil burner is based. Whether Franklin applied this principle to a lamp is still an unanswered question. But we may well give him tentative credit for it. We know he was interested in lighting and that he invented a lantern for the city of Philadelphia. Tradition often proves to be based on facts.

Miles Patent Lamps

What we now call a whale oil lamp is an " agitable " lamp patented in 1787 by John Miles, a button maker of Birmingham, England. His patent did not cover vertical wick tubes, which indicates that these were known at the time. It did mention, however, that one or more tubes could be used, of any shape. What he patented, and what was the " talking point " of his invention, was an oil tight font. It could be agitated without spilling the oil. Miles' invention came at a favorable time ; people were looking for something better than low, flat lamps that spilled oil easily and distributed the light poorly. A tall lamp with a centrally located burner would be much better and would be popular if it could be sold at a price the average citizen could pay.

Plate 21 Two models of prehistoric lamps. *Upper:* Sandstone lamp c. 20,000 years old, with a moss wick. (Model by Kenneth Mathews) *Lower:* Chalk lamp from an English mine, c. 10,000 B.C. (See pages 1 & 17)

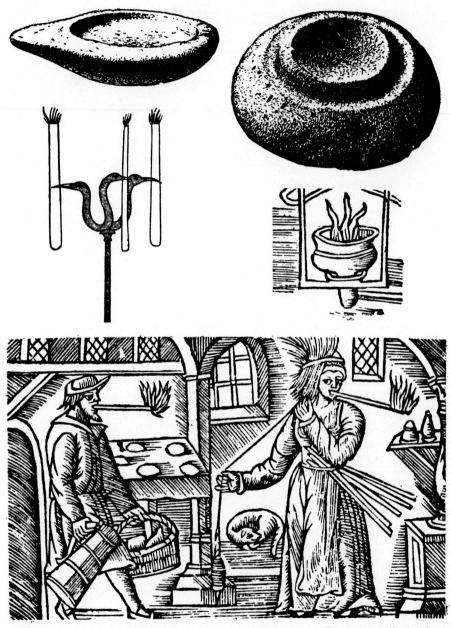

Plate 22   Top: Prehistoric stone lamps.   *Middle left:* Etruscan splintholder
c. 600 B.C.   *Middle right:* Blubber lamp, with a peg, used by Goths. *Bottom:*
Early use of splints in Sweden, 15th century. (See pages 1, 4, 6 & 51)

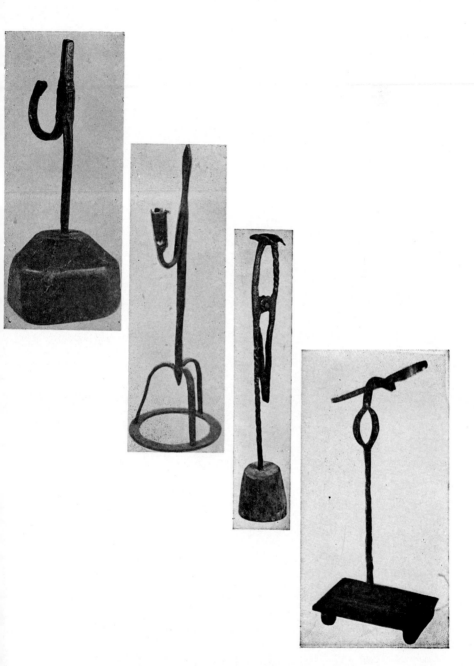

Plate 23 *First :* Splint or rushlight holder. *Second :* Rushlight holder. *Third*
& fourth : Rare types of splintholder (See pages 6 & 108)

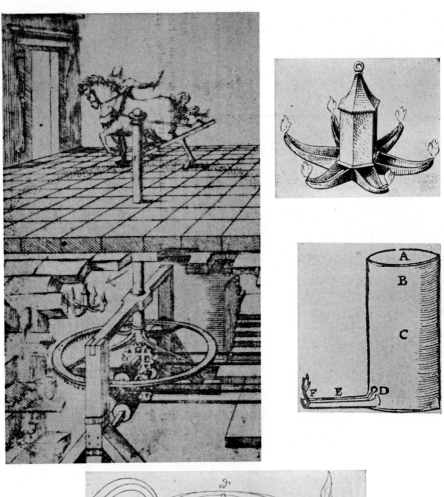

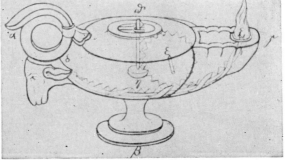

Plate 24   Top left: 16th century engraving showing lamp.   *Top right:* Enlarged drawing of the lamp.   *Middle right :* Cardan's sketch of his lamp, 1555.   *Bottom:* Lamp with automatic feed for wick, cir. 200 A.D. (See pages 10, 22, 35, 38 & 85)

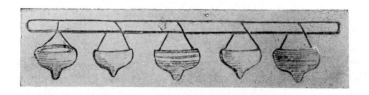

Plate 25 Float lamps (See pages 12 & 15)

Plate 26 Two float lamps, two old glass lamps for drop burners and a later type with burner in place (Courtesy of The Science Museum, London) (See pages 15, 44 & 52)

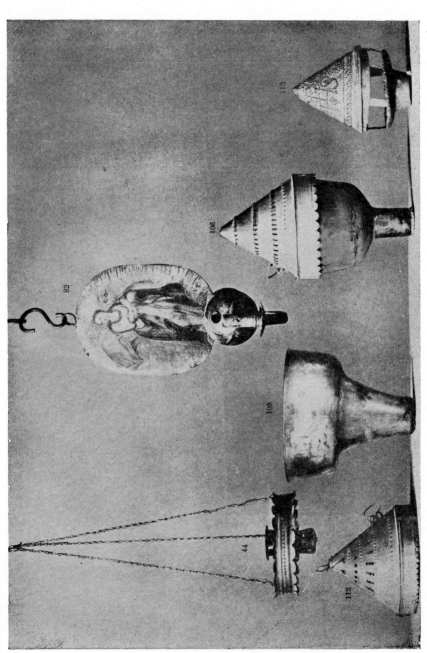

Plate 27 Nos. 44, 105, 106 and 113 are float lamps, No. 122, a cover; and No. 82, a sconce (See page 15)

Plate 28 Crusie with a wick channel of unusual form and a notched half-bail to adjust angle of lamp towards the wick (Catherine Otley Collection) (See page 20)

There was no drawing with Miles' patent but one has been made from his detailed description. This description does not include a "peg" but one must have soon been added, for the oldest Miles Patent Lamp we have is a peg lamp. We have evidence that his lamps were a financial success, for he is listed in the Birmingham directory for 1801 as a "gentleman." No man could be so designated at that time if he worked with his hands or owned no real estate. Miles had invented, made, and sold a lamp for both general and common use. His lamp was never improved technically except by the addition of a screw type burner and there is evidence that this appeared on later models.

British Patent Number 3184, issued in 1808 has: "......the wick tube held in place by means of a screw as in Miles lamps." Another patent issued the same year is for "an improved agitable lamp." These patents prove that after twenty-two years, both Miles and the descriptive name he gave his lamps were remembered.

Miles lamps were advertised and sold in this country at least as early as 1800 but usually as "Patent lamps." Four lamps with a name plate stamped "Miles's Patent" are owned by members of the Rushlight Club. The oldest is a tin peg lamp; the others are made of cast brass and are about eight inches tall with rather small fonts. (Plate 47)

Whale Oil Lamps

A whale oil lamp is commonly accepted to be a lamp with a whale oil burner but there is some disagreement about the details that make a burner with vertical wick tubes a whale oil burner. For all practical purposes, however, a whale oil burner is one that: (1) screws into the font; (2) has one or more round wick tubes, usually slightly tapered, all extending below the burner plate and (3) has slots for adjusting the wick. The burner described in Miles' patent specifications was not a whale oil burner but some later models were. The term "whale oil lamp" is generic and there are specific names for many lamps with whale oil burners, such as peg and petticoat lamps, lens lamps, etc. These have fonts of different shapes and other features of design which distinguish them. When a lamp has the general details given above and has no other specific name, it is safe to call it a whale oil lamp. It is something more than a lamp with a vertical wick tube. See Plate 44.

Tests on Whale Oil Burners

Professor Edwin B. Rollins, former editor of *The Rushlight*, is an engineer. He has tested whale oil lamps with one, two, and three wick tubes to determine their candlepower and has made many separate measurements using different lamp oils. Their averages are as follows: a 2-tube burner gives 2.25 times as much light as a single tube burner, a 3-tube burner gives 3.86 times as much light as a 1-tube burner. To put it another way, if the 1-tube gives 1 candlepower, the 2-tube burner will give 2¼ candlepower, and the 3-tube burner, 3 7/8ths candlepower. The 3-tube burners were both those with the tubes in a straight line and those arranged in a triangle; little difference in their performance was found.

The type of glass lamps, some with handles, made for drop and cork burners, may be seen in Plate 45 and elsewhere. Some of these are called sparking lamps, doubtless because they gave so little light—only a spark. Others are known as lacemakers' lamps, a most elastic term. They all have one thing in common, being free blown—that is, neither pressed into shape nor blown into a mould. Lamps with simply a hole for an all-metal burner are probably the oldest. Those with a short neck were for cork disc burners. How old each of these types is must be left to glass specialists but it appears that they are at least as old as 1780. Peg lamps with with spherical fonts are much older.

Priests' Lamps

This is an important example of an old lamp with a vertical wick tube. Hough comments in *Bulletin 141:* "Priest's lamp. A very old French Specimen (c. 1550) supposed to have been used by priests for night visitations. It has a drawer for flint and steel." Similar lamps are shown in Plates 39 and 42. Some are equipped with a draft protector, making it a small lantern, while others are held on standards and even have bulls-eye lenses. These were doubtless for use in drafty places in the church, including lecterns. We are not sufficiently acquainted with the details of these lamps to offer an opinion on how much the burner is like a whale oil burner.

Peg and Petticoat Lamps

As a group not much can be said about peg lamps, as the peg is the only distinctive thing about it. This is attached to a wide variety of lamps and these are described in their particular groups. Peg lamps are very old. The blubber lamp illustrated in Plate 22 is from *The History of the Goths and the Vandals*, Upsala, 1555. The glass float lamps shown in ring type chandeliers in medieval miniatures are still older and some of these chandeliers with similar lamps still exist in Germany. Cheapness and convenience are the reasons why peg lamps have been used over so long a period. The oldest are the glass float lamps followed by spherical glass lamps for drop burners (Plate 26). The term peg lamp is an Americanism and its use may have been limited to the northeasterly states as they were called stump lamps in some parts of the South. In England, where they were made before they were here, they were called socket lamps by lampmakers, that is, lamps to be inserted in the sockets of candlesticks. Glass peg lamps are more numerous in antique shops than metal ones but these are not all true pegs. Pressed glass lamps with unusually long pegs, especially if these are roughened or notched, were intended to be fused or cemented into a glass or metal base. Tin peg lamps are rather rare and include the types used in carriage lanterns. Other very rare specimens are made of brass, pewter, silver and even china. Those of pewter and china are the rarest.

Petticoat lamps usually have pegs and may thus be included in this group. English dealers called them "stand and socket" lamps and their users, "skirt lamps." The common type is made of brown lacquered tin but a few made of pewter have been noted. One made of any other metal would be rare indeed. See Plate 9, 2nd shelf, and 48.

Peg and petticoat lamps commonly have whale oil burners, as that is what they were originally equipped with. Some pegs have the twin tapering tubes for burning fluid but usually they have been converted to use this illuminant. Others with Sandwich glass fonts seem to have been provided with fluid burners at the factory. At least one with a kerosene burner has been noted. For some reason petticoat lamps with fluid burners are quite rare.

Pig Lamps

These lamps are doubtless so called on account of their porcine appearance—the first ones may have had four legs. Some of them have a small pan over one of the burners that has been called a spice burner. They have also been called guest lamps, which is ridiculous, since they are entirely unsuited for domestic use. Collectors disagree about their age, what oil they burned and the purpose of the little pan. They are usually made of lacquered tin and have three rather large wick tubes, not of the whale oil burner type. Wicks of this size are likely to smoke badly unless they are carefully adjusted and no slot in the tube is provided for this purpose. See Plate 50. The thought has been advanced that these were made to burn kerosene and are no older than 1865. We cannot be sure about this but we can be sure that they were made to be used in shops and factories where a little smoke would not be so objectionable. They are quite rare.

Canting Lamps

These lamps are designed to burn the last drop of oil in the font. In some of these, this adjustment is done by hand as needed, while in a few others it is effected automatically. In either case this is done by suspending the font on pivots or trunnions and shaping or suspending the font so that the oil can be made to flow towards the wick. The hand-adjustable type consists of a cylindrical oil container pivotted axially. The wick tubes, round or flat, extend tangentially from the curved surface. These wick tubes will be vertical at only one position of the font and at varying angles at other settings. See Plate 43, left.

One fully automatic type is illustrated in the three photo-

53

graphs in Plate 53. This lamp functions very efficiently, as its owner has demonstrated clearly in the pictures with the help of the line in the background. When the font is full of oil it hangs as shown at the left. As the oil is consumed the burner end gets lower and lower until it assumes the position shown at the right. This must be a patented lamp although it is not so marked. Not may of them could have been sold, however, for they are rare. Possibly they came on the market about the same time that coal oil was spouting in Pennsylvania.

Lens Lamps

Lens, bull's-eye, or reading lamps are usually made of pewter and have two lenses. But there are many exceptions. These lamps are commonly assumed to focus the light as a reading glass focuses the rays of the sun. This is not a fact, but they must have provided better illumination for some purposes or there would not be so many of them. A lens lamp functions similarly to the water-filled globes used by lace makers and cobblers. Experimenters with these lamps and water lenses do not agree on a theory for the success of these devices, but they concede that the lenses, whether water or glass, do help. There is a limited diffusion through the lens and the effect of flickering seems to be reduced.

A lamp apparently made for a doctor has but one lens, but this is on an adjustable arm and its distance from the source of light can be varied according to the law of conjugate foci. The light of this lamp could be focused to cover a small area at higher intensity.

There are lamps with one, two and four lenses. At least one of these is made of tin and doubtless there are others made of brass. See Plate 44.

Lard Oil Lamps

In 1840 the cost of lamp oils was almost prohibitive for the average family. The United States Government paid $1.57 a gallon for sperm oil for lighthouses. Private citizens paid up to $2.50 a gallon. Whale oil was much cheaper, but the price was the only thing about it that was popular. Sea elephant oil must have found a ready sale at 75¢ a gallon, as the herds along our Pacific coast were practically exterminated. An advertisement in the *Boston Traveler* in 1841 claims: "It gives a clear light and will bear a large flame without smoking." In Europe, conditions were similar or worse and such oils as rapeseed or colza, mustard seed, oil from nuts and others were used by those who could afford them. Colza oil was tried here for lighthouses. In the states between the Alleghanies and the Mississippi, there were five million inhabitants and the price of lamp oils must have been prohibitive except near navigable rivers. They had plenty of lard for grease lamps but no cheap oil for whale oil lamps. Lard is the most nearly fluid of the common fats but it cannot be burned satisfactiorily in a common wick tube lamp. The country was eager for a cheaper lamp oil and it found it in lard oil from "prairie whales" or hogs and in "burning fluid." Special lamps had to be devised to burn each of these new illuminants.

A lard oil lamp is not any lamp in which lard oil *can* be burned; it is a lamp specially devised to burn it. The feature common to all these lamps is some sort of a heating device to warm the oil and keep its viscosity low. Most lard oil lamps have flat wicks but this is not the touchstone. Flat wicks often made ot two thicknesses of cotton flannel were used. The theory of these heat conductors was that they heated the oil in the font and thus assisted capillarity to lift the oil to the wick tubes, where it was hottest. But any heat drawn from these tubes cooled them off a bit, so that it seems like robbing Peter to pay Paul, as the following expert opinion indicates (these comments on lard oil lamps are taken from the U. S. Patent Commissioner's Reports for the years 1840—1844):

1840 Lard or lard oil is not mentioned.
1841 By the aid of Chymistry the West will soon find one of their greatest exports to be oil .... lard is converted into stearine for candles .... also oil from cornmeal. A gallon of (lard) oil can be afforded for 50¢. Sperm oil sells for $1.50 (wholesale?).
1843 Lard oil sells for 75¢ a gallon at retail.
1844 The separation of lard into oil and candlestuff is now accomplished by pressure applied in a certain manner. Thus far no hand lamps have been invented to burn (solid) lard near the top of the wick.
    Devices for conducting the heat of the flame downward into the lard are still resorted to, though it is entirely nugatory to bring a conducting body into the flame as its refrigerating effect renders such lamps useless. If placed above, it is awkward and soot collects.

From 1840 to 1860 lard and lard oil were popular illuminants. Many lard burning lamps were patented during this period but it is doubtful if many of them were a success. Solid lard, as before noted, will not burn well unless some

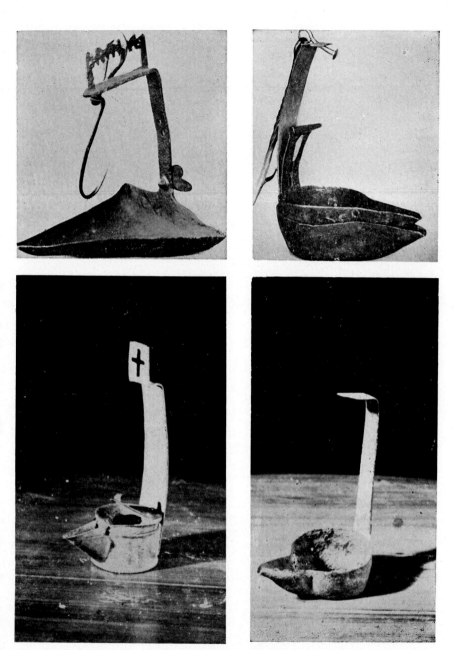

Plate 29 Upper left: Lower pan of double crusie. *Upper right:* Double crusie. *Lower left:* Tin double crusie. *Lower right:* Single crusie (National Gallery of Art, Index of American Design) (See page 20)

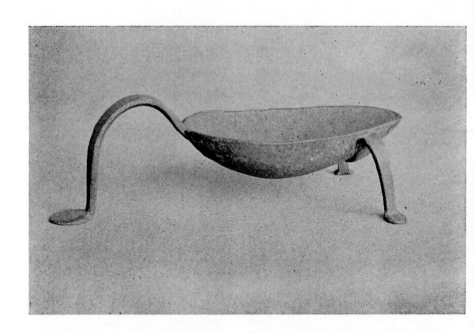

Plate 30 Upper: Rare crusie on legs. *Lower:* Witch lamp (National Gallery of Art, Index of American Design) (See pages 20, 22 & 23)

Plate 31 Rare crusie with cover, on a stand (National Gallery of Art, Index of American Design) (See page 21)

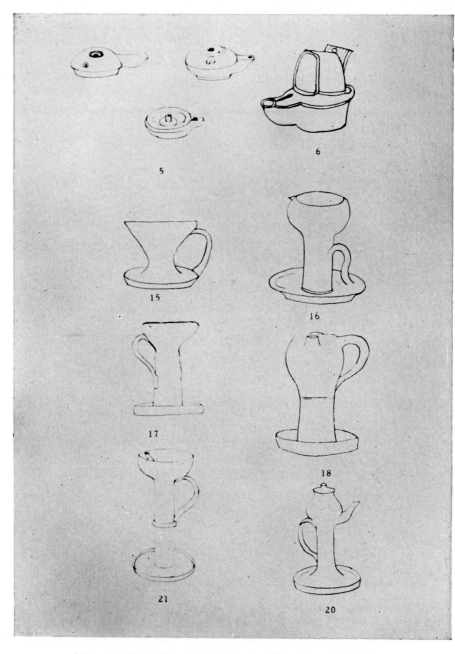

Plate 32 Primitive pottery lamps (See pages 24 & 27)

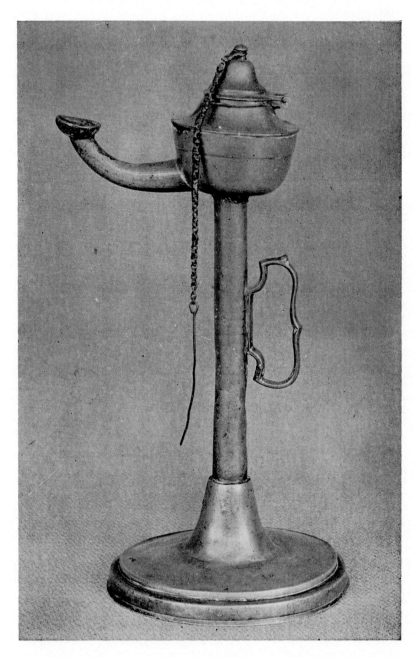

Plate 33 Moorish (?) pewter spout lamp or rabbis' lamp (National Gallery of Art, Index of American Design) (See page 30)

Plate 34 Sixteenth-century kitchen showing lighting devices
(See page 35)

Plate 35 Sixteenth-century kitchen showing lighting devices
(See page 35)

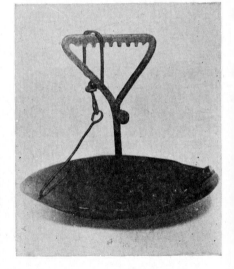

Plate 36 *Upper:* Clay pan lamp; wick-hole lamp (rare); semi-spout lamp; two blown glass lamps for drop burners. *Lower left:* Pewter Betty. *Lower right:* Odd-shaped crusie to which a wick tube has probably been added (See page 37)

of it is within an inch of the top of the wick. A solid fuel is not therefore adapted to be burned in a tall lamp. Smith and Stonesifer, however, patented a lamp in 1854 that was equipped with a screw-driven piston which forced lard up into a small chamber around the wick (Plate 51). If given a turn of the screw occasionally, this lamp might have functioned quite well. Apparently they did, as they are fairly common in collections and more significantly, they show signs of use. Small hand lamps equipped with heating devices for melting solid lard or warming lard oil were not, in the opinion of the U.S. Patent Commissioner (1844), much of a success, although many of them were sold. At this time, the terms " lard " and " lard oil " seem to have been used interchangeably and we are not always sure which product is referred to. It is nowhere so stated, but evidently solid lard would have to be melted to get it into the font of a tall lamp ; this would burn well as long as it remained fluid. The Commissioner was discussing lamps which had at most two small flat wicks. These would not produce heat enough to keep the lard melted, except possibly in summer. Larger and more costly lamps with Argand burners generate more heat and it is possible that they would burn solid lard satisfactorily. The simple heating conductors commonly found on small hand lamps are a continuation of the flat wick holder down into the oil, such as the one shown in Plate 44. This is a typical uncomplicated lard oil lamp. Lamps with a more elaborate heating system are described later with other patent lamps. Many of these were patented but few of them seem to have been sold. Considering the quantity of lard oil sold after 1845, a disproportionately small number of lamps with any kind of heating system beyond that supplied by whale oil burners is to be found in shops and collections. This suggests that much of this oil was burned in the whale oil lamps that everyone had. The extension of the wick tubes below the burner plate would have some heating effect. For additional information on patented lard and lard oil lamps the reader is referred to an article in *The Rushlight* for February, 1954 by Professor Edwin B. Rollins.

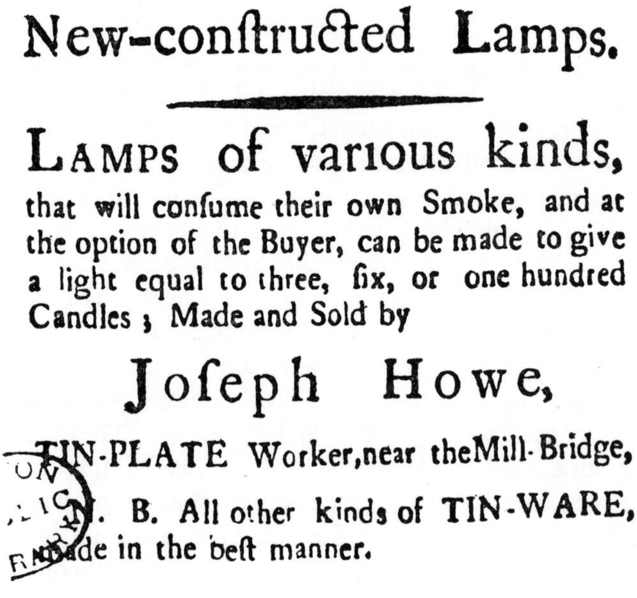

New-conftructed Lamps.

Lamps of various kinds,

that will confume their own Smoke, and at the option of the Buyer, can be made to give a light equal to three, fix, or one hundred Candles ; Made and Sold by

Jofeph Howe,

TIN-PLATE Worker, near the Mill-Bridge,

N. B. All other kinds of TIN-WARE, made in the beft manner.

Fig. 4 Advertisement for Argand lamps from a Boston newspaper, 1787

Burning Fluid Lamps

Camphene Lamps

Burning fluid was an early nineteenth-century name for a mixture of alcohol and turpentine. This was burned in lamps with tapering, divergent wick tubes, erroneously called camphene lamps. According to the first edition of *Webster's Dictionary*, published in 1828, camphene is another name for turpentine. Camphene lamps had Argand burners.

Not all fluid lamps have burners with twin tapering wick tubes. A few have been noted with long brass wick tubes extending from two to five inches above the font to keep the flame away from the body of the lamp. These lamps were evidently designed to burn some volatile liquid but we are not sure whether in was burning fluid or gasoline.

Different men in different countries doubtless discovered that a suitable mixture of turpentine (which is the same as spirits of turpentine) and alcohol burns with a whiter flame than oil lamps. The difficulty was to get these two liquids to mix. The secret was to have not over 2% of water in the mixture, otherwise it separates out. If shaken to effect a mechanical mixture temporarily, the flame sputters badly. Various methods were eventually used to secure this nearly anhydrous mixture.

The first writer in this country to call attention to what was later called burning fluid was Professor Robert Hare in an article published in *The American Journal of Science and*

Arts in 1820, but it was over twenty years before burning fluid became at all popular. The increasing cost of whale and sperm oils stimulated a demand.

According to the United States Patent Office records, Isaiah Jenning was the first to patent what was later called burning fluid. In his patent of October 6, 1830 he specified " a mixture of alcohol and spirits of turpentine—mix and agitate them that they may mix together ; let them stand a while, and the alcohol will combine with a small quantity of turpentine and the remainder will be separated. Draw off the small portion of alcohol and turpentine combined and it will be ready for use ". Henry Porter was the first of record to give this mixture a name. His patent of April 8, 1835 calls it " Porter's Patent Portable Burning Fluid " and it was extensively advertised and sold under that name.

The use of burning fluid increased with the increase of the cost of lamp oils but it was not until about 1850 that we read much about it in the newspapers or that there was a demand for " safety lamps " such as Newell's. It continued to be used until displaced by kerosene.

Burning fluid had a bad reputation for explosiveness. Insurance companies forbade its use but the trouble was more in the habits of its users than in the fluid itself. A generation used to kerosene would probably have had little trouble. Whale oil lamps could be filled, spilled and dropped without danger. Fluid lamps could not.

There are two kinds of fluid lamps: those designed for it and whale oil lamps fitted with new burners. The first group is likely to be made of pressed glass of a frustum shape for stability. The other group includes fonts of any material and shape in which whale oil lamps are found. The lamps shown in plate 56 are all of the latter type. The burners may be pewter or brass or brass tubes soldered into a pewter base. The wick tubes are tapered and there is no slot for adjusting the wicks, which are smaller than those in whale oil lamps. They are compressed at the top by the tapered tubes. The caps originally attached to the burner plate by chains are often missing. These are thought to have been for extinguishers and to prevent evaporation. They fit very loosely but they may have helped. See Plate 56. The writer has experimented with these lamps using anhydrous wood alcohol and redistilled turpentine. Using three to four parts of alcohol to one of turpentine, a bright flame is produced. If the flame is too colorless, add more turpentine; if too smoky, more alcohol. The flame is particularly sensitive to drafts, which cause it to flicker and smoke but under favorable conditions a twin burner fluid lamp will give about three candlepower, which is more than any two-burner whale oil lamp will provide.

There were many patents for burning-fluid lamps. Newell's was the most popular in New England. In this lamp the wicks were enclosed in a fine silver-plated wire mesh attached to the underside of the burner plate. A similar mesh was soldered to the collar of the font. Rarely do we find one of these lamps with both intact, or more than a trace of the silver plating, which indicates that they had seen actual use since the mixture has a strongly corrosive effect. These meshes were of little practical value inasmuch as they did not surround the flame as in a miner's lamp but it was a good talking point and large numbers of them were sold. In fact this was the only patented burning-fluid lamp that seems to have been sold in any considerable numbers.

Many strange combinations of alcohol, benzene, turpentine and other materials were patented around 1850. Patent No. 54,696 calls for a mixture of alcohol, naphtha, white oak bark, slippery elm bark, alkonet root, camphor, saltpetre and salt. Another, No. 59,797, calls for 40 gallons of gasoline,

8 pounds of sulphur, 100 pounds of rusty nails and a bushel of onions.

Camphene lamps that burned turpentine without added alcohol were patented both in England and in this country. In England they were sold under the trade names of Vesta and Paragon lamps. (See Ure's *Dictionary* and Grove and Thorpe's *Chemical Technology*, Vol. III.) United States patents were issued to Jennings, Carr, Dyott, Horn and DeGuinon. These are lamps of the Argand type and can be indentified by their nameplates. If this is lacking, reference must be made to patent records. They all have some device intended to increase the draft and the supply of air to the flame. They are rare.

Vapor Lamps

Vapor lamps have also been called spirit lamps because they burned volatile fluids such as gasoline. All lamps burn a self-generated gas but the wick in most is in contact with the flame. In vapor lamps gas is drawn up by the wick and vaporized, so as to issue from a series of small holes, where it burns like illuminating gas. In operation, the burner was heated by allowing a little of the fluid to flow from the burner and lighting it, or it was heated in a separate flame. After that the heat from the flame was supposed to keep the burner hot enough to vaporize the fluid brought up by the wick. This principle works well enough on larger lamps such as the torches formerly used by circuses, outdoor markets and others, also in gasoline stoves for camp use, but apparently the relatively small vapor lamps were not a success, since few of them are found in antique shops. They are identified by the fact that no wick is visable and there are small holes in the burner for the escape of the gas.

Patent Lamps

Patent lamps are hard to discuss except in either general terms or in detail. Collectors are not usually interested in the mechanical minutiae of patent specifications and very often when these specifications are followed and the lamp is put on the market, it does not resemble the model supplied the Patent Office. Most patent lamps are marked with the name of the inventor. Lamps with glass fonts are sometimes an exception but this information may be stamped on the burner plate. Not many pictures of individual lamps are available but a large number of them are shown in Plate 17. After a century or more most patent specifications are out of print and these examples of patent lamps are invaluable for identification purposes. See Plate 44

During the thirty years following the establishment of the United States Patent Office in 1870, thirty-four patents for lighting devices and fuels were issued. The first patent for a lamp was granted to John Love of South Carolina for a tallow lamp but we have no further details. Other patents were for candles and candlesticks, and for methods of producing or burning illuminating gas, including two issued to David Melville of Newport, Rhode Island. Among the early nineteenth century patents was one for a " reflecting and magnifying lantern " and another for a method of splitting and shearing horn for lanterns. A patent for a lamp was issued to James Mallory of New York in 1812 and a second to Winslow Lewis of Boston but we have no details of either. The oldest patent lamp for which we do have any detailed information, is the Howe Nurse Lamp and Warmer, issued to William Howe of Boston in 1812. This was advertised in the *Columbian Sentinel* on January 16, 1813.

Howe was a member of a family of lampmakers who had made parts for the first lanterns installed on the streets of Boston. Howe claimed for his lamp that it heated milk for infants and water for shaving. It could be used as a lantern; its handle served as a candle holder and there was a box with flint, steel and tinder in the base. One of these lamps of the original model as pictured in advertisements was owned by a former member of the Rushlight Club. This is the oldest patented lamp so far discovered and is probably unique. Later models are more common.

There are nearly fifty patent lamps from the Rushford Collection illustrated in Plate 17. This does not include several lamps identified only by their trade names such as, "Firefly," "Little Buttercup," and "The Burglar's Horror." Included in the first group of patents are the Newell Patent burning-fluid lamp, previously described, the Zuriel Swope Patent of 1860, the Samuel Davis Patent of 1856, the Delamar Kinnear Patent of 1851 and others. Of all these the last seems to have been the most popular.

The Kinnear Patent Lamp

The best evidence of the popularity of this lamp is the number of them still existing in museums and private collections and the fact that they can still be found in shops. This popularity may not have extended beyond New England but it probably did. The writer has burned these lamps and believes them to give the most light and to be the

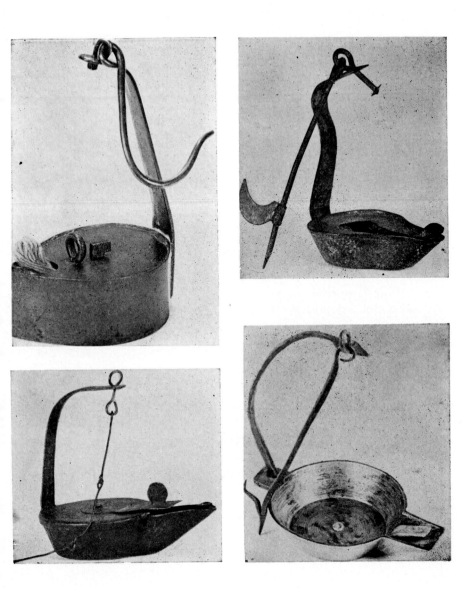

Plate 37 Three typical Betty lamps and an Eastern type Betty (See page 37)

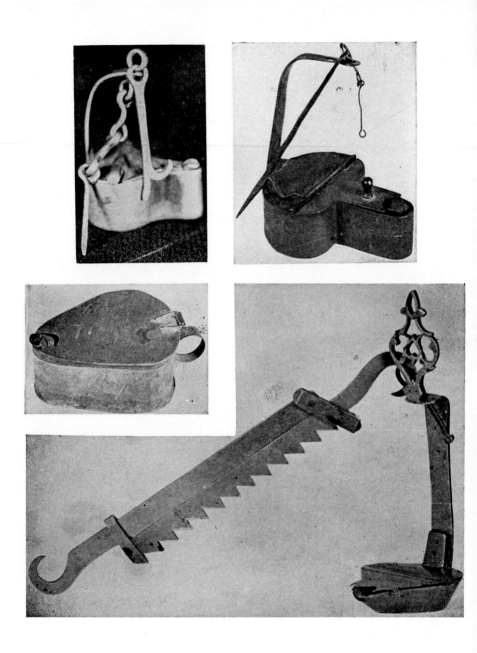

Plate 38 Miniature pewter Betty, 2 inches tall, and three other Betties, one with trammel (See page 37)

Plate 39 Numbers 13 and 81, priests' lamps on stands with lens;
others, Cardan lamps (Von Benesch Collection) (See pages 39 & 51)

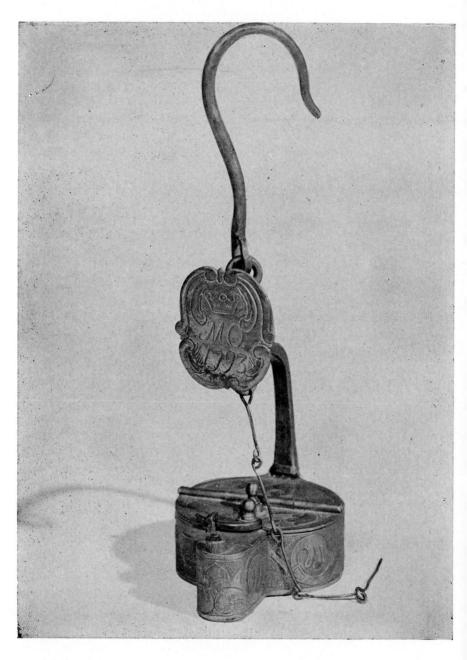

Plate 40 A rare cast brass Betty. From the Near East (?) (Howard Stone Collection) (See page 35)

Plate 41   A very rare semi-porcelain lamp with wick-tube (Julius and Frances Daniels Collection) (National Gallery of Art, Index of American Design) (See pages 37, & 44)

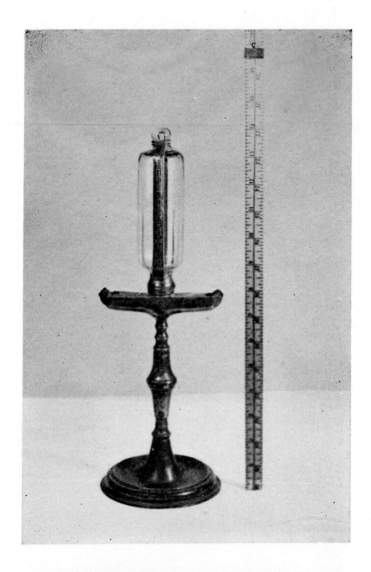

Plate 42   Top: Time lamp   *Bottom:* Priest's lamp
(Mathews Collection)   (See pages 42 & 51)

Plate 43 *Top :* Canting lamp and Kinnear patent lamps. *Bottom :* Wick-hole lamp (Helen Brigham Hebard Collection. National Gallery of Art, Index of American Design) (See pages 44, 53 & 65)

Plate 44   Top left: A whale oil lamp.   *Top right:* Single bull's eye lamp, tin. *Bottom left:* Pewter lard oil lamp   (Helen Brigham Hebard Collection) *Bottom right:* Davis patent lamp   (National Gallery of Art, Index of American Design)   (See pages 50, 54, 57, 63 & 65)

most generally satisfactory of any of the relatively cheap lard-oil lamps without chimneys. They sold for from 67 ¢ to $ 1.25. Lamps with Argand burners were better but they cost more. Kinnear lamps gave only about half as much light as Argands but they cost very much less and had no breakable chimney. Another cause for their popularity was that they were well-advertised—at least in Massachusetts—by Ufford, whose name appears on the nameplate. Kinnear is not mentioned. There are two groups of Kinnear lamps: those with the Ufford nameplate and those with no nameplate at all. If the inventor made and sold any of his lamps in the Central States, we have no evidence of it. Presumably Ufford either bought the patent rights or was licensed to manufacture them. The lamps sold by this firm commonly have an open-work cast iron base but there is at least one exception. See Plate 43.

Other individuals or companies besides Ufford must have made Kinnear lamps since there are a number of them in local collections with no nameplates. Most of these have a square pan base as shown in the patent drawing but there is at least one of these lamps with a round saucer base. It has been surmised that these square based lamps were made outside of New England. It is hard to see how any successful action for infringement could be held against a local tinsmith for making and selling them as there was nothing new in any of Kinnear's claims, except possibly the "peculiar form of the font." Two things contributed to its success. It had a wide wick extending down into the oil and it was well advertised. The lamp shown in Plate 44 has the same essential features but it is not a Kinnear Patent lamp.

The Zuriel Swope Lamp (1860)

This lamp, shown in Plate 50, is the most picturesque of

all patent lamps, with its heat collector rising from the flat top of the font like a drooping lotus flower in an Egyptian wall painting. It is hard to understand why a patent for this lamp was ever granted as its essential features were patented by Winslow Lewis years before. The author has never seen one of these lamps that showed signs of much use but this is far from persuasive evidence. Whether used or not, a collector is fortunate to come upon one, as they are rare. Doubtless some of them have been preserved on account of their intriguing appearance.

Other patent claims are briefly:

M. B. Dyott: An improvement in turpentine or camphene lamps having (1) an air regulator; (2) two discs at the top of the wick; (3) the mode of regulating the light and (4) the peculiar construction of the wick tube.

Ellis Archer claims a lamp for burning solid lard. It had "a hollow button to be filled with lard" and also an Argand burner.

Isaac von Bunschoten claimed a lamp for burning rosin oil— a turpentine distillate. It was similar to the Vesta lamps sold in England. There is one of these in the Rushford Collection.

Horsford and Nichols patented a lamp for "guarding against accidents in lamps burning volatile fluids. We claim the combination of the safety wick tube, the perforated safety chamber (etc.)".

F. H. Southworth claims "the peculiar form of the wick holders ... arranged for burning lard by converting it into oil by conductors of heat in contact with the flame."

66

Many lamps have only the date of the patent stamped on them. To identify them, the " Abridgement of Patent Specifications " must be consulted. Having found the name of the inventor and the patent number, if it is not too old, a full copy of the specifications with drawings can be obtained from the Patent Office. The large libraries may have them also.

The Davis Patent Lamp, 1856

The printed directions which originally accompanied these lamps say that " the wick should be loose enough to be easily regulated up and down to give the light wanted. If the lard in the lamp be cold and there is no warm lard to start it, hold the lamp upside down and apply a lighted match to the burner until it gets hot, then set the lamp down and put a little cold lard in the lid around the wick. The wick should be made of Canton flannel doubled and put into the burner with a wire." The two wicks accompanying the lamp were made of this Canton flannel, 4 by 1½ inches, folded lengthwise with the " fur " side in and loosely stitched. (See plate 44)   —A. H. H.

The Rumford Lamp

There is one popular lamp that must be included in any discussion of patent lamps, although its inventor never patented it. Like his contemporary, Benjamin Franklin, he did not believe in patents designed to restrict the use of improvements in the arts. Today these lamps are known to collectors as Rumford lamps, but as yet there is little evidence that they were so called in the first half of the nineteenth century when they were most popular. Luke Hebert (*The Engineer's Encyclopedia*, London, 1842) credits Count Rumford with the invention and says: "it is equal to any, whilst at the same time its construction is extremely simple." On the other hand, Oliver Byrne (Appleton's *Dictionary of Machines*, Philadelphia, 1851) calls it a "study lamp" with no mention of its inventor. See Plate 54.

Count Rumford was born Benjamin Thompson of Woburn, Massachusetts, in 1753. He died in France in 1814. Thompson was a Tory who fought against us in the latter part of the Revolution. At the end of the war he was knighted by King George III and was later invited by Prince Maximilian of Bavaria to join his court. In 1791 he was created a Count of the Holy Roman Empire and chose his title from Rumford, the old name for Concord, New Hampshire, his one-time home. We do not know when he invented the lamp that now bears his name but it was probably between 1790 and 1800.

In Rumford's *Sixteenth Essay*, published in London in 1812, he writes:

" My attention was first turned to (lighting) in the year 1789 when I was employed by his Serene Highness ......In lighting up these spacious establishments, I first learned how much room there was for improvement in the art of illumination. I took pains to make myself thoroughly acquainted with lamps and the causes of their imperfections......I caused to be constructed more than one hundred lamps (all differing from each other, more or less). The results of these experiments enabled me to contrive two lamps, for different purposes, which came into very general use in Bavaria; but as both of these are inferior to the lamps I shall recommend in this Essay, I have not thought it useful to publish a description of them.

(With many omissions) " A near view of the naked flame of an Argand lamp is quite insupportable as is well known. The only way the flame can be masked without a great loss of light, is to cover them with...... thin white silk, gauze and various other substances....... One of my first attempts to put these principles into practice, was made in the year 1800. Argand lamps with several burners were suspended from the ceiling, (and later in Paris) the illuminator was constructed which I presented to the National Institute of France on the 24th of March, 1806."

These illuminators are very rare; they are here mentioned for their curious interest and to make identification possible.

The other lamp described in his *Essay* is his " Portable Lamp. " In Rumford's complete works there is a detailed description and sketches of the lamp that later became so popular. As often happens, some of the features described were found to be unnecessary refinements, since it was not used as a hand lamp but on the table. These lamps were popular because they were cheaper than Argands but gave more light than whale oil lamps. In addition to their relatively low cost, they had the following advantages: a wide wick for the period; a wick raiser; a shade that reflected the light downward toward the table; a chimney to increase the draft around the flame; and an oil font on a level with the top of the wick-tube. This font was small and cast a small shadow but it held little oil. When good lamp oils cost from $1.50 to $2.50 per gallon, lamps of this type were not burned except for a specific purpose such as reading or writing. There are two (or more) models of these lamps, one English and one French. The first is more sturdy and specimens are found in perfect condition; French models may be more artistic but they have not worn well. See Plates 54 and 55.

Argand Lamps

From the earliest historical times down to the later part of the eighteenth century there was little improvement in lamps. They still gave about the same amount of light per wick. What little improvement there had been in over 20,000 years was in the direction of multiple burners, convenience and better distribution of light. These are worthy achievements but they do not solve the major problem of the lamp, which is to give light. At the end of the seventeenth century lamps gave little more than one candlepower per wick, except at the expense of a smoky flame. The lamps invented by Greek engineers were probably never used until Carden adopted the constant level feed for the oil. There was still no improvement in candlepower per burner. In this respect, the best lamps available in 1750 were no better than the first clay lamp with a wick channel. But shortly afterward this condition was dramatically changed.

In 1780 Ami Argand, a Swiss chemist was in Montpellier, France, where he had gone to install a system of distillation which he had devised. While there he was dissatisfied with the lamps then in use and invented an entirely new burner. We are not to assume that this was the first time he had given any thought to it or even that he was the first to think of getting a current of air into the inside of a flame. Benjamin Franklin had the same idea and experimented with it briefly and inconclusively as noted below.

In 1784, Thomas Jefferson, who was then in France with Franklin, wrote to Charles Thompson, Secretary of the Continental Congress as follows:

> "There has been a lamp called a cylinder lamp lately invented here. It gives a light equal to six or eight candles. This improvement is produced by forcing the wick into a hollow cylinder so that there is a passage of air though it. This idea had occurred to Dr. Franklin a year or two before but he tried his experiments with a rush, which not succeeding, he did not prosecute it. The fact was that the rush formed too small a cylinder; the wicks used on the cylinder lamps are an inch in diameter. They sell for two guineas."
>
> (N.Y. Hist. Coll. 1878, p. 196)

Jefferson doubtless received this information directly from Franklin, who had tried a rush with the pith removed as a crude sort of hollow wick. Argand rolled a flat wick into a cylinder and enclosed it between two brass tubes. The inside tube extended downward from the burner and opened on the base of the tube supporting it. Air was drawn up through this (first) tube by the heat, into the inside of the flame where it was most needed.

According to Micheaux' *French Biographies*, Argand first exhibited his lamp to M. Maquer of the Academy of Science in 1783. The Academy later reported: "A single one of these lamps gives as much light as twenty tallow candles." This exaggeration was doubtless prompted by the hitherto unequalled brilliance of the flame. Micheaux says that Argand made his first lamp in England. Possibly this was

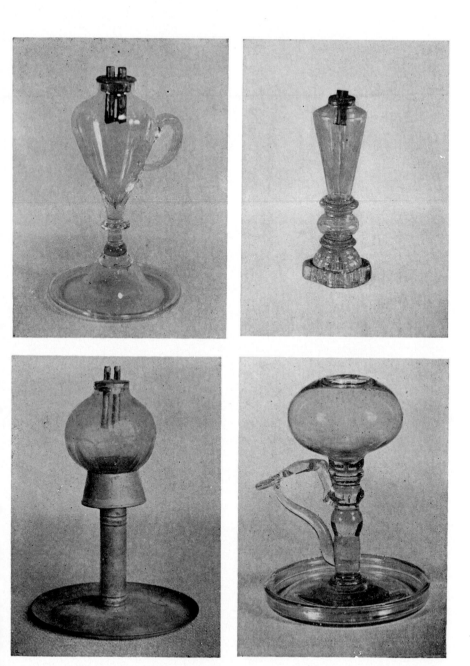

Plate 45 Four glass lamps for drop burners (National Gallery of Art, Index of American Design) (See pages 44 & 50)

Plate 46   Glass peg lamp with drop burner on stand (Howard Stone Collection. National Gallery of Art, Index of American Design)   (See page 45)

Plate 47 Miles patent lamp (Quentin Coons Collection) (See page 49)

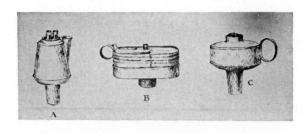

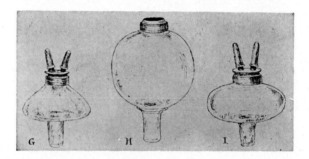

Plate 48   Peg lamps   (Sketches by Arthur Hayward, from *The Rushlight*)
(See page 52)

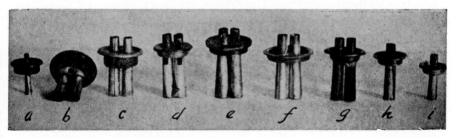

Plate 49   Drop, cork and whale oil burners   (See page 46)

Plate 50 Top: Swope patent lamp. *Bottom:* Pig lamp. (Julius and Frances Daniels Collection. National Gallery of Art, Index of American Design) (See pages 53 & 65)

Plate 51 Smith and Stonesifer patent lamp. Here the burner is at the side and the reservoir has a screw plunger to force the fuel upward (National Gallery of Art, Index of American Design) (See page 57)

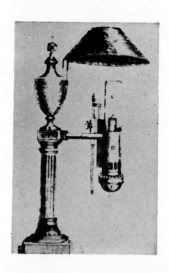

Plate 52 Top: Argand lamp of 1788. *Bottom:*
Tin Argand lamp cir. 1800 (National Gallery of
Art, Index of American Design) (See page 74)

the first one of the symmetrical type. But he did patent his lamp there and a copy of it is available. It was issued in 1784.

> "A lamp so constructed as to produce neither smoak (sic) nor smell and to give considerably more light than any lamp hitherto known, by converting the smoak into flame, by causing a current of air to pass through the inside of the flame and by producing another current of air on the outside of the wick by means of a chimney." (Patent No. 1425)

While Argand was in England, troubles for him were developing in France. Lange, the Royal Distiller, improved Argand's cylindrical chimmey by reducing its diameter sharply just above the wick and, on this showing, and his influence at Court, a patent was issued to him for the complete lamp. In addition, an opportunist named Quinquet began to advertise and sell Argand lamps under his own name. He was so successful that they were commonly known in Paris as Quinquets. Franklin so named them in his famous "Daylight Saving" letter. Lange's claim to any share in Argand's patent was eventually disallowed but we do not know what happened to Quinquet. The events leading up to the French Revolution made conditions unfavorable for any new device not connected with war. Argand was unable to contend against these adverse circumstances and returned to Versoux, where he died shortly afterward.

The oldest known Argand lamp is an English model made by Boulton & Co. in 1784. It was brought to America by Thomas Jefferson. This silver lamp is illustrated in *Antiques*, Vol. XV, page 187. A similar lamp is shown in Bradbury's *Old English Plate*, page 395.

73

The oldest known picture of an Argand lamp of the French type with a fountain feed is shown in Plate 52 taken from the *Journal des Luxus und Moden* for September 1788. A good picture has one advantage over the lamp itself— none of the parts will be missing. This German-made lamp has a shut-off valve for use when the lamp is filled, a rack and pinion wick adjuster, a cylindrical chimney and a fountain feed.

It is unlikely that many Argand lamps were made in America in the eighteenth century but there is competent evidence that one or more were made in Boston in 1786. Deacon Joseph Roby, a tinsmith, advertised in the *Massachusetts Sentinel* that he had them for sale. A later advertisement states that he " has the directions for making them from Mr. Williams who has just returned from France." It is noted in the Town Records that " a Mr. Williams " did indeed return from France at this time.

Astral, Moderator

and

Other Lamps with Argand Burners

There are few lamps with Argand burners that are so named today; nearly all of them are known by the name of the inventor who has improved the oil delivery system or by some descriptive name. Thus we have astral, sinumbra, moderator, mantel-arm, students' lamps and Rochester burners. The first considerable improvement on Argand's continental model was by a relative and associate, Bordier-Marcet. The English models described earlier could not have been practical. These were much like a modern Rochester burner, which requires an oil as thin as kerosene for successful use. We do not know what oil the English used in 1784. Whatever it was, it was either too heavy or too expensive for general use even among those who could afford silver lamps.

Astral Lamps

Argand lamps with a fountain feed were unsymmetrical and the font cast a large shadow. Bordier-Marcet in 1808 patented "Une Apparel Astral," a chandelier so named because the "light comes from above, like a star." This was a wheel type, with a ring-shaped font and several Argand burners. In 1810, he patented a table lamp with the same shaped font and a central burner with a shade. This was the original of the astral lamps we see today. The purpose of the ring-shaped font was to permit the burner to be set at oil level. The font was thin both for good distribution of light and for a nearly-constant oil level. The burner had the newly-invented Phillips' spiral wick raiser, which has been used ever since. After thinner oils became available, the ring font was replaced by one of turnip shape and it is this type that is usually found today. Internal draft is provided either by a tube extending to the base or by a series of holes around the bottom of the font. See Plates 57 and 58.

Sinumbra Lamps

A sinumbra lamp is one with a ring-type font of special cross section designed to cast as little shadow as possible. Phillips' original model of 1820 had a font of wedge-shaped cross section and his spiral wick-raiser. Sometime later, someone patented, or at least made and sold, a lamp with a curved cross section and it is these that are commonly seen in shops and collections. Both these and astral lamps are frequently embellished with glass prisms and pendants. Such lamps are most attractive but one is rarely found complete with chimney, shade and all the prisms. See Plate 57.

Solar Lamps

These lamps differ very slightly from astral lamps, the difference being a saucer-shaped draft deflector just above the top of the wick. This detail was patented, presumably in England, some time prior to 1848, inasmuch as the American edition of the *En yclopedia of Domestic Economy* published in that year says that it is a lamp with a solid round wick, the draft being deflected by a metal cap. "Lamps of this construction with simple wicks, give no smoke when used with the best oil and the flame is exceedingly bright." The writer has one of those lamps. The turn-up button is stamped "Pat Applied For" but no further data. The U.S. Patent Commissioner mentions solar lamps in his report for 1843. They were made by Cornelius & Co. of Philadelphia, and existing specimens are usually marked so, together with the name "Solar." These lamps have Argand burners and usually a plain cylindrical support or column.

Mantel-Arm Lamps

Technically these lamps are copies of Argand's French models. They have been incorrectly called astral lamps but they were advertised as mantel lamps in both Boston and New York. They were popular as a functional mantel decoration from 1820 to 1850. They usually came in sets of three; two with single arms for the ends of the mantel and one with double arms for the center. Made in England and France they frequently bear the nameplates of local dealers. Being sturdily constructed of bronzed brass, they were kept on Victorian mantels long after they ceased to be used as a source of light. See Plate 57.

Moderator Lamps

These lamps were the most popular of all costly prekerosene lamps. They were not so named because they were used by moderators but because the flow of oil to the wick was moderated and controlled by a tube of small internal diameter. Oil was forced into this tube by a large spring in the base attached to a piston—a sort of force pump. This mechanism is so designed that it can be set into a vase of almost any shape or material. These vases are found in a variety of materials but the most handsome are made of china or other pottery. Moderator lamps are identified by the large key at the base of the burner, which winds up the compressing spring in the base. The button for adjusting the wick is smaller and is higher up on the other side. See Plate 59.

Carcel Lamps

This lamp, named after its inventor, was patented in France in 1800. A patent for a similar lamp was later issued to Diacon in England. Both lamps, and others of the same type, have a spring driven pump to deliver oil from the font to the top of the burner. In point of performance it was the best of all pre-kerosene lamps, as long as it was in good working order. Various contemporary comments and advertisements suggest that they needed frequent cleaning and overhauling to keep them in good condition. Possibly the oils used in the first quarter of the nineteenth century tended to harden about the moving parts. The New York Gas Company formerly used a Carcel lamp to provide a uniform standard flame for measuring the candlepower of its illuminating gas. A member of The Rushlight Club, Mr. F.C. Doble, has one of these lamps that has been repaired and is now in good running order. The driving spring winds up like a clock. This model has a twin cylinder pump, which moves very slowly, forcing oil through a pipe up to the wick. It is hard to understand why this would get out of order easily but a century ago people were not as familiar with mechanical devices as we are today. See Plate 60.

Oleostatic Lamps and Rochester Burners

These lamps provide a non-mechanical method of supplying oil to the wick, based on the hydraulic principle that the liquids in a U-shaped tube balance according to their specific gravities regardless of the different capacities of the arms. A liquid of high specific gravity was put in one tube or arm and oil in the other, which had a larger diameter. There was nothing to get out of order but for some reason they were never as popular as the lamps just decribed and they are very rare. Even a photograph is hard to find.

The only Argand lamps now in common use where electricity is unavailable are descendants of the Rochester burners of the late century and of his original lamp in the form of student lamps. The former has a flame spreader which is lacking in the latter, and also a larger wick. Student lamps are still made and sold. They now have a spiral wick-adjuster and a removable oil font with an automatic valve at the bottom, permitting it to be removed for filling. The Rochester burner is really a descendant of the English type of Argand lamp. They still have a rack and pinion wick-raiser. The flame spreader is the only technical improvement. Since kerosene became available, this type of lamp has been most popular.

The Menorah, Hanukkah and Sabbath Lamps

These three lamps are peculiar to the Jewish religion and culture. The Menorah is the oldest and in its present form is much like the "golden candlestick" described in the Book of Exodus, with the exception that candlesockets have now replaced the earlier lamps. This is a synagogue lamp. The Hanukkah (various spellings) is a lamp for home use, modelled in its essentials from the Menorah but varying in its significance and in its form, which has varied greatly according to available materials and local skills. With a single exception, it should not be used for any practical purpose. It is a ceremonial light, as is the Sabbath lamp, but the latter may be used as a source of light for reading or general illumination.

The Menorah

This is the first and only lamp to be described in any ancient literature. The description will be found in Chapters XXV and XXXVII of the Book of Exodus (900–1000 BC). It was to be made of "pure gold beat out with the hammer," with the six branches and the central shaft holding lamps. These branches and the shaft were to be embellished with bowls, flowers and knops, "the bowls like unto almonds," "under every two branches, a knop,"

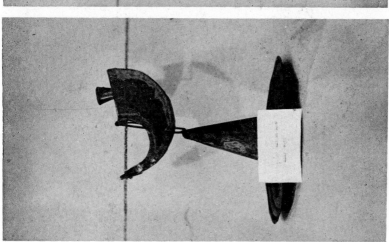

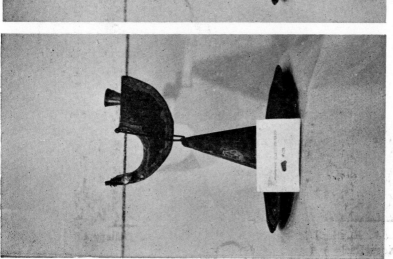

Plate 53 Automatic canting lamp in three positions: full, half full, and empty, *from left to right* (Toalson Collection) (See page 54)

Plate 54 Rumford lamp, English type   (National Gallery of Art, Index of American Design) (See page 68)

Plate 55 Rumford lamp, French type (National Gallery of Art, Index of American Design) (See page 68)

Plate 56 Four burning fluid lamps (National Gallery of Art, Index of American Design) (See page 60)

Plate 57   Top left: Sinumbra lamp.   *Top right:* Astral lamp.   *Bottom left:*
Double arm mantel lamp.   *Bottom right:* Single arm mantel lamp   (National
Gallery of Art, Index of American Design)   (See pages 76 & 77)

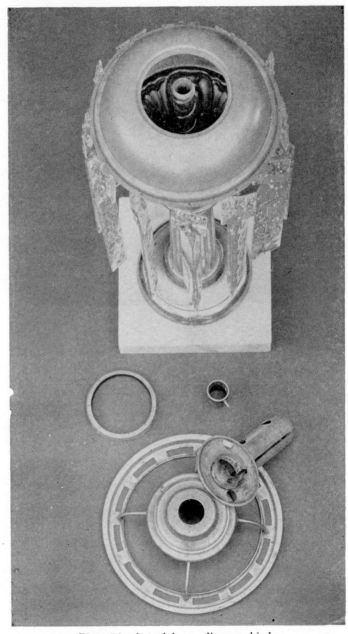

Plate 58 Astral lamp disassembled
(National Gallery of Art, Index of American Design)
(See page 76)

Plate 59 Moderator lamps (*Left :* National Gallery of Art, Index of American Design. *Right :* Science Museum, London) (See page 77)

Plate 60   Glass Carcel lamp   (British Crown Copyright; Science Museum, London)   (See page 79)

"and for it, seven lamps with snuffers and snuff dishes." Different translations of these texts use different words but it is evident that "bowls" did not refer to the oil containers since these are mentioned separately with no further description. A sixteenth-century artist's conception of the Menorah is taken from the Geneva (breeches) Bible, first published in 1587. See page 82. Other murals and carvings show the Menorah with a square base. These are the best pictorial evidence we have.

Josephus, the Jewish historian, who was born about 37 B.C. and who must have seen many Menorahs, describes them as follows:

> Over against the table......was set a candlestick of cast gold, hollow within, of the weight of a hundred pounds. It was made with its knops, lillies, pomegranates and bowls, which ornaments amounted to seventy in all. It terminated in seven heads in one row; these branches carried seven lamps.......

This is historical written evidence but it is subject to the many hazards and errors of translation. This "candlestick" was a lamp stand. There is a Latin and a French word for this but no English word. Words have different meanings at different times and places, so that today we can never be quite sure what they meant two thousand years ago. The revised version of the Bible says it was made of beaten gold; Josephus says it was cast. Both state or imply that it stood on the floor. The original Menorah was destroyed by Antiochus Epiphanes about 163 B.C. but Jerusalem was recaptured by Judah Macabees and a new one was made. Two hundred years later the Temple was again despoiled by the Emperor Titus and the Menorah was brought to Rome. The triumphal procession displaying this and other sacred objects is depicted on one of the panels of the arch erected by Hadrian sixty years later. The Menorah here shown has a heavy square base and, compared with the human figures in the foreground, seems to be about five feet tall.

THE CANDLESTICKE.

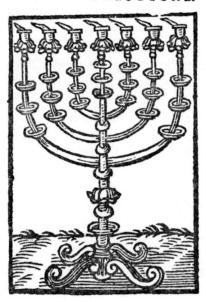

Becaufe the fafhion of the Candlefticke is fo plaine and evident, it needeth not to defcribe the particular parts thereof according to the order of letters. Onely whereas it is faid in the 34 verfe that there fhall be foure boules or cups in the Candlefticke, it muft be underftood of the fhaft or fhanke: for there are but three for every one of the other branches.

Alfo the knops of the Candlefticke, are thofe which are under the branches as they iffue out of the fhaft on either fide,

31 ¶ Alfo

Fig. 5 Menorah, from Breeches' Bible

Unfortunately for our special interests, the Bible describes only the lamp stand in any detail. Presumably the lamps were shallow pan lamps with the wick resting on the bottom, nearly covered with oil. The lamps shown in the picture from the Geneva Bible suggest wicks of this kind. Certainly the artist, who made this woodcut four hundred years ago, knew more about such lamps than we do.

Although the traditional form of the Menorah is as

82

described above, it is quite possible that, under some circumstances, the lack of materials and skilled artisans would force a compromise; there would have to be makeshifts, using such facilities as were available. It would not be surprising if there have been Menorahs made of clay. Some of them may still exist.

The Book of Exodus not only gives us the first known description of a lamp (stand) but it also tells us who made it. When Moses went up to Mount Sinai to receive the tablets of the law, he was also commanded to build the tabernacle and to make all its vessels and furnishings. "Thou shalt make an ark of acacia wood......thou shalt make two cherubims......thou shalt make a candlestick and the lamps to give light. And see that thou make them after their pattern as hath been shown thee......And Jehovah spoke to Moses saying: 'I have called Bezalel, the son of Uri......to work in gold and silver and brass......'". Bezalel (there are different spellings) was the grandson of Miriam, who was Moses' sister. It is nowhere definitely stated that Bezalel made the great golden candlestick, but since he is the only metal worker mentioned, we can be as sure as we are of many things that he made the first lighting device of which we have a written description.

The Hanukkah

The Menorah is a synagogue lamp and tradition forbade its use in the home, but a lamp of similar design—the Hanukkah could be made for secular use as well as sacred, during the Festival of Lights, which lasts eight days. The Hanukkah has eight lamps (or candle sockets) and one more, the Shamash or Server. These eight lamps may not be used for any common household purpose but the Shamash may; it

83

is the first lamp lighted and the others must be lighted from it. " In the synagogue, the Hanukkah maintains the erect position of the Menorah. Not so in the home where it was modified so that it could be placed on a window sill or hung on the wall. The hanging lamp requires a back to support it and on this are designs such as palm trees, grapes, the Lion of Judah, the Menorah, the Crown of the Law, etc.; sometimes the figure of Judith holding the head of Holofernes and a dagger. Hanukkah lamps today use candles and are in common use in Jewish households. In the olden days, lamps burning oil were used, and many of these had a high degree of craftmanship and symbolism. The metals used in their construction are pewter, brass, silver, often completely or partly gilded." (*Jewish Encyclopedia.*)

In a local collection there is a rare brass Hanukkah of a transitional type. There are the usual nine candle sockets and in addition, each one is provided with a thick cover pierced with a hole for a wick, so that the candle sockets could be filled with olive oil and there would be nine lamps burning instead of candles. See Plate 63.

Sabbath Lamp

This is primarily a functional lamp although its use is supposed to be limited to the Sabbath. It is usually a chandelier or suspension type, with six wick-channel lamps arranged in a senary form in emulation of the six-pointed Star of David. It is lighted in Jewish homes at the beginning of the Sabbath. There may be more than six lamps similarly arranged but that is the usual number. If a modern Sabbath lamp is compared with the sixteenth century lamp sketched in Plate 24, it is evident that they are technically the same. In either case the purpose of the lamp was to give a good light for all occasions and the multiple wicks would provide this. Sabbath lamps were commonly made of brass as they are today but a few may be found made of pewter or silver.

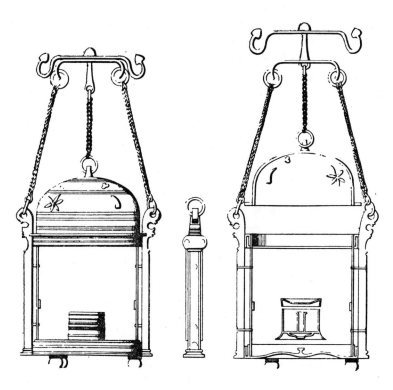

Fig. 6 Lantern from Herculaneum

Lanterns

A lantern is a shelter for a lamp or a candle, to protect it from drafts. It is an outdoor utensil. We do not know who made the first one or when, but they are doubtless very old. The Greeks were no better informed, as in the second century Alexis of Thurii commented: "Whoever invented the first lantern, to carry when he set forth at night, was certainly very careful of his hands." He must have referred to the danger from sparks and hot pitch, when a torch was carried. Whatever lights were carried by Diogenes in his search for an honest man or by Hero to guide Leander across the Hellespont, torches, not lanterns, seem the most probable, iconography to the contrary. A lantern would have been too costly and would have given too little light. Quite a number of them have been excavated at Herculaneum. A drawing of one is shown on page 85 and it has a vertical wick tube as has been noted earlier. The frame is made of bronze and there were two curved horn panes. The owner's name is engraved on it. This and others like it are the oldest lanterns we have.

Lanterns can be divided into two groups, portable and fixed. The latter are classified in various ways but commonly by their position, such as ship's lanterns, street lanterns, carriage lamps, headlights and hall lanterns. An advertisement of 1754 reads: "Four dozen glass lanterns, proper to illuminate a house on publick occasions." Portable types can be classified by their materials, shape or the purpose for which they were made. There are pierced, horn, bullseye, wooden and globe lanterns.

In a summary of all lighting devices mentioned in seventeenth-century Essex County (Mass.) inventories, fifty-one lamps are listed and forty-five lanterns. This suggests that they were quite as necessary as lamps in colonial life.

Someone has suggested that the oldest lanterns were open only at the bottom. The French called them *sourde* lanterns. The next improvement would be to cut or punch holes in the sides so that some of the light would be shed laterally and not downward. Such a lantern would be cheap and durable and it would not be surprising if they had been used for a thousand years, although we cannot prove it. The lantern that signaled to Paul Revere waiting across the Charles River has been erroneously supposed to be of this type but we can be sure that no such lighting device was ever hung in the belfry of the Old North Church, because they give too little light. Nevertheless these pierced lanterns are named after this famous silversmith and patriot and the term is well established. See Plate 61 and the collection of lanterns in Plate 19.

Kerosene or Coal Oil Lamps

The kerosene lamp is the best oil-burning lighting device the world has ever known. Crude petroleum was known to the ancient Assyrians. Pliny mentions it and fifteen hundred years later, Bellenden called attention to certain "quhair streames of oulie springes." In North America, it was first reported by Joseph d'Allion, a Franciscan monk (Sagard, *History of Canada*, 1632) and in the next century Peter Kalm, the naturalist, located several oil seeps in Pennsylvania.

The success of petroleum as an illuminant depended on the development of drilled oil wells, refining methods and a new burner. Prior to 1860, shale oil produced by roasting shale enjoyed a considerable popularity and large quantities were distilled. Although the existence of crude oil in Pennsylvania and elsewhere was well known and it was collected in limited quantities, it was not until 1861, when Colonel Drake's first "spouter" came in, that it could be economically collected and refined. Almost at once all other lamp oils became obsolete and expensive but a new burner was needed to take full advantage of this new illuminant. In 1866 there were 194 distilleries in the United States, with an output of 28,000,000 gallons annually. New burners could not have been commonly available at this time and doubtless much of this new oil was burned in whale oil lamps.

We do not know who invented the common kerosene burner. No one has traced the steps by which a burner with a flat wick, a spur turn-up, a dome-shaped deflector

Plate 61 Wooden lantern (National Gallery of Art, Index of American Design) (See page 87)

Plate 62 Hitchcock lamp (Kenneth Mathews Collection) (See page 90)

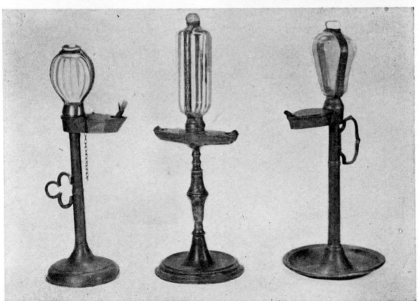

Plate 63   Top left: Hanukkah with wick plates; burns either candles or oil.
(Rollins Collection)   *Top right:* Silver taper holder.   (Mathews Collection)
Bottom: Three time lamps   (Mathews Collection)   (See pages 40 & 84)

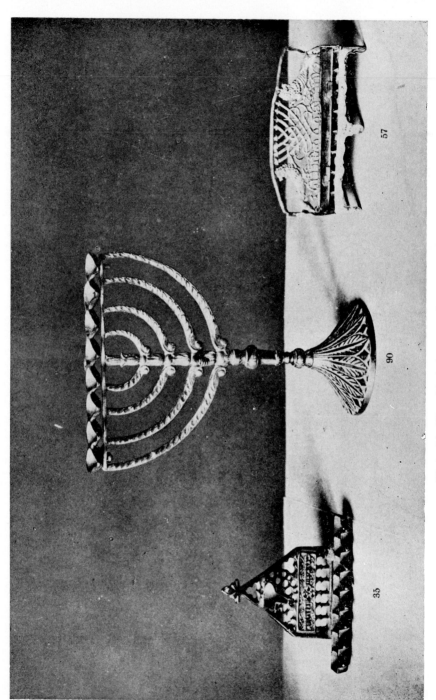

Plate 64 Hanukkah lamps. (See page 83)

with a chimney were made practicable. The draft deflector is the important feature of the kerosene burner. This may have been suggested by a similar detail in the solar lamp. The best evidence of the origin of the former is found in the records of the Supreme Court, *Carleton vs. Boker, 1 72.* It is here cited that the lamp best suited to burn petroleum distillate without smoke was first introduced into England about 1856. This was commonly known as the Vienna burner, which suggests Austria as the country of its origin. " It is conceded that two burners were in use (in the U.S.) before 1858. The Steuber burner of 1856, made in considerable quantities in Utica, and the Vienna burner. " The name of the inventor of this important burner was not brought out at the trial.

In 1860 solid round wicks were used on practically all hand lamps. These had no wick turn-ups or chimneys and could be tipped and carelessly handled. The new kerosene lamps were "top heavy" and the chimneys were easily broken, so burners were patented for use without chimneys, such as "Danforth's Atmospheric Coal-oil burner which needs no chimney." But as the quality of the chimneys improved and people were more careful of them, the need for such burners diminished. Kerosene lamps are collected today, not for their burners, but for their decorative fonts. These are found in both glass and pottery, in table models and suspension types. See Plate 20. Anyone interested in these is referred to the 1955 edition of Freeman's *Lights on Old Lamps*, which has many authentic pictures from contemporary catalogs.

The Hitchcock Lamp

This is the latest lighting device that can be properly classed as an old lamp, since it is a little less than a hundred years old. These lamps have flat wicks and they were designed to be used without chimneys, as they have spring-driven blowers to provide the necessary draft. A lamp of this type was patented in England in 1840 and in the United States in 1860. After passing through other hands, this and later patents were acquired by Robert Hitchcock. These lamps must have been a success as they were advertised in *The Delineator* in 1895 and a new one was purchased in Canada within the past ten years. In outward appearance they resemble the Rochester Burners of the nineties but they have flat wicks and are much heavier, due to the spring-driven blower in the base.

Mr. Kenneth Mathews of Stockton, California has experimented with it. He reports: "It does indeed burn without smoke and gives a bright white light. Before it is lighted the draft from the blower can hardly be felt but it is adequate." See Plate 62.

It has always been justifiably assumed that all blower-type lamps were made by Hitchcock & Co of Watertown, New York and that none of them had any provision for chimneys, but a letter and photographs from Carleton W. Brown of Fenton, Michigan, offers strong evidence to the contrary, if not absolute proof. He has a lamp which is stamped on the burner "N.Y. May's New Ideal Lamp. Pat'd June 10, 1884." He also has two other lamps whose burners are designed to hold chimneys. These are shown in Plate 96. One of them definitely has springs to hold a chimney on the burner, and the turn-up is stamped "Approved Hitchcock."

The Candle Group

Webster's dictionary defines the word "candle" as : "(1) A light made of tallow or wax" and "(2) A slender cylindrical body of tallow or wax with a cotton or linen wick." The first definition is a broad one covering an archeologist's grouping of any combination of pitch or fat with some vegetable material. These crude devices developed into candles, but they were not candles in the commonly accepted meaning of the word, as described in (2) above. The multivolumed *Oxford English Dictionary* defines it as : "A (usually) cylindrical body of wax, tallow or the like, formed around a wick of cotton or flax or formerly the pith of a rush." A rushlight is a rush drawn through melted fat once ; a rush candle is a rushlight dipped many times until it is cylindrical like other candles. It is of course impossible to say just when it becomes a candle but the distinction between the two is clear. Whatever candle-like devices the Greeks and Romans had, it is unlikely that they were candles as defined above. Whenever the word "candle" is used here without qualification, it means a candle of a substantially modern type and not *lebacei, cerei, funalia,* links, flambeaux or rushlights. In a true candle the purpose of the wick is to consume the fat ; in cruder devices, as in the case of a rope soaked in fat, the purpose of the fat is to help burn the wick.

In general, we cannot learn the details of any ancient objects unless we have either the objects themselves, a good description of them, or a picture. We have lamps of all ages from 20,000 B. C. down to the present, but no candles and few descriptions or pictures. "Candle-makers' instruments" were unearthed at Herculaneum (destroyed in 79 A. D.). The oldest surviving candle-like device may be a fragment found at Vaison near Avignon, attributed to the first century A. D. Here we are dealing with archeological terms and do not know if these "candles" conform to the previous definition. We have one good description of a candle dating from early in the Christian Era. Varro (116–27 B. C.), says in his "book" on the derivation of Latin words, *De Lingua Latina:* "From 'candela' comes 'candelabrum,' to which these burning ropes are attached." (*Candelabrum a candela ex his enim funiculi ardentes figebantur.* V. 119). This makes it clear that candles in Varro's time or earlier, were ropes smeared with tallow, wax, or pitch. Atheneus (3rd century A. D.) confirms this. "Candles are made of ropes (or cords) covered with wax." "Candles" of this type would be carried in the hand. No candleholders of the socket or pricket type have been found among the many utensils excavated in the Mediterranean area. We can therefore be reasonably certain that candles of anything like modern types were unknown as late as the Roman Empire.

Any discussion of the age of candles usually brings out an unidentified quotation to the effect that in the time of the first Christian Emperor, Constantine, the streets of Constantinople were lighted with candles until it was as bright as day. This is an approximation of what Eusebius, the father of church history, says in his *Life of Constantine.* More fully and accurately it is: "At Easter, at the time of the Holy Night vigil, night was turned into day by pillars of wax and by torches shedding their light." There is nothing to indicate that these "pillars of wax" had a

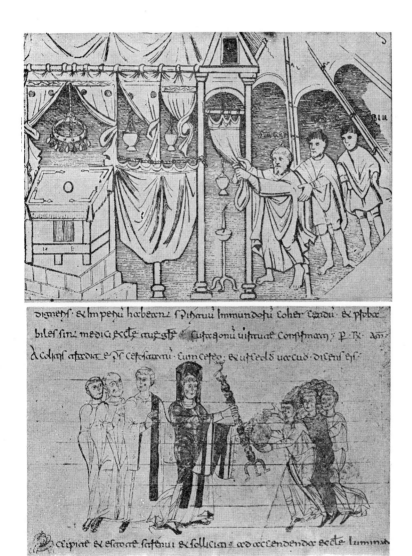

Fig. 7 Top: Aaron and his two sons at the entrance to the sanctuary. Aaron is drawing aside the veil. A candle with pricket candle holder is shown near him. 7th century A. D. *Bottom:* Ordination ceremony. The short taper on the large candlestick may have been used because it was the type of candle used by the early Christians. 11th century.

single wick but they evidently differed from torches.

Pictures are the best evidence we have of the existence and the appearance of objects that no longer exist. They also enable us to date those objects within variable limits. The oldest book pictures we have are the illustrations in ancient manuscripts, some of which are as old as the third century A. D. These pictures are called miniatures, not because they are small but because they were *miniated* with a red lead pigment, minium. These pictures are factual, as the artists—particularly the older ones—painted what they saw. If there is a candle in one of these pictures, we can be sure that it is at least as old as the painting. One limitation is that the kind of lamps or candles depicted are those used in churches and are not domestic types. The frontispiece of this book is the sole noted exception.

The oldest picture of a candle the writer has been able to find is the one shown on page 93. The original is a seventh-century miniature in the Bibliotheque Nationale. The candlestick with a burning candle is shown standing just inside the sanctuary. As Aaron, followed by his two sons, Nadab and Abihu, draws back the veil, the draft causes the flame to flare. If we credit the artist with this bit of realism, we can believe he has shown us what a seventh-century candlestick and candle looked like. There is other evidence of the form of candlesticks. There is a silver pricket type in the Walter's Collection in Baltimore. It is similar to the one shown in the miniature and is said to date from the fifth century. Other candles are shown in the *Exultet Roll* painted in the eleventh century. One of these miniatures shows a very large candle being lighted from a taper wound around a long staff. Another, on page 93, shows a short taper on a tall candlestick. This picture illustrates the ceremony of admission to the priesthood, and this old type of candle may have been used because it was the kind used by the earliest Christians. These are the burning ropes mentioned by Varro and the *cereis* of Apuleis.

After the so-called fall of Rome, Latin gradually ceased to be a spoken language, but it was preserved by the clergy and by scholars. The Church had its own terminology and in the tenth century and later, the word *candela* meant a lamp. Du Cange cites many examples of this in his *Clossarium*. For example:

Candelae breves aenae	Small bronze lamps
Candelae olei redundare	The oil in the lamp ran over
ex oleo de candela	Lamp oil
(Papal bull, 1047.)	

The story of the English king, Alfred the Great (died 900 A. D.), and his time candle has both human interest and technical detail. This account is found in Asser's *Life of Alfred*. Asser was his chaplain and the Bishop of Exeter.

"When Alfred our king had thus set all in order, he vowed that half the service of his mind, would he, by day and night alike...render unto God. But by night, because of darkness and by day by reason of rain and clouds, he could not rightly tell the hours for his prayers, he set himself to think how with God's help he might at fixed times keep his vow. And when he had thought upon this he invented a useful device and of good wit. He bade bring wax and weigh it in the balance against pennies, until so much of it had been added as balanced seventy-two pennies. Then he bade make thereof six candles of equal weight, and that each should have twelve divisions marked upon them. So when this device had been completed, six candles were burned... throughout the twenty-four hours before the holy relics of many a Saint of God, which were ever with him, whithersoever he went."

"Some times these candles would not last through-out a whole day and night, even unto the same hour at which they had been lighted the evening before. This by reason of the drafts which blew in by the windows and doors of churches and in the many chinks in the stones and cracks in the partitions. Yea and through the rents in tents, these drafts made the candles burn away over soon. The King there-fore thought how he might hinder this and he sought out a wise and curious craftsman and bade make of wood and horn a full fair lantern. Now cowhorn is white and a thin sheet is clear as glass, so when the lantern was reddied and a candle set therein, it gave as much light as if it were outside and it was hindered by no drafts, for there was a door of horn to it. By this device then, the six candles, one after the other, burnt without stay for the twenty-four hours, neither more or less."

Because Asser gives the weight of wax in the candles and their approximate length, we can estimate the amounts of wax in each candle and have some idea of their diameter. These would be rush candles, as it is doubtful if cotton was available in England in the tenth century and flax or linen make very poor wicks. A silver penny of King Alfred's day—and long afterwards—weighed a pennyweight or a twentieth of an ounce troy measure. Since there were seventy-two pennyweights for six candles, each weighed twelve pennyweights. This would be nearly a cubic inch of wax: enough to coat a rush the size of a large plastic knitting needle and form a rush candle nearly half an inch thick. Rush wicks do not need to be snuffed and they burn longer. The *Oxford Dictionary* quotes: "Why should a rush candle burn longer than a cotten one? (1708)."

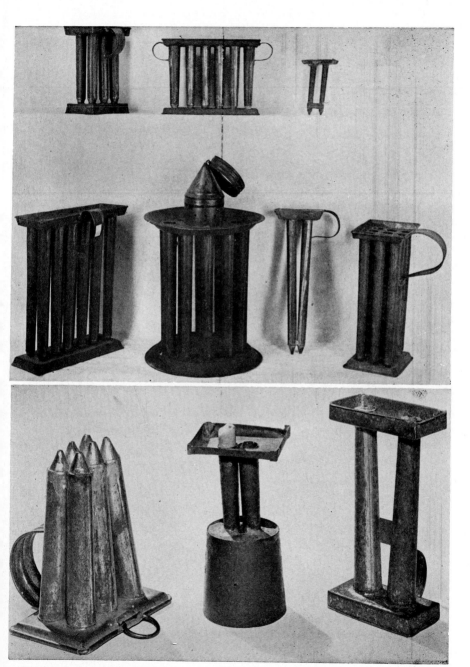

Plate 65 Top: Candlemolds. (Carleton Brown Collection). *Bottom:* Three small candlemolds, height less than four inches (See page 106)

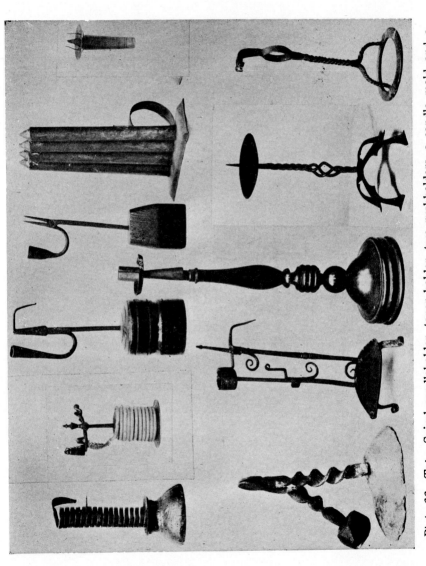

Plate 66 Top: Spiral candleholder, taper holder, two rushholders, a candle mold and a saveall. *Bottom:* Rush holder, Alpine candle (?) or torch holder. (From the Brown, Hehard and Science Museum Collections) (See pages 109, 113, 116 & 118)

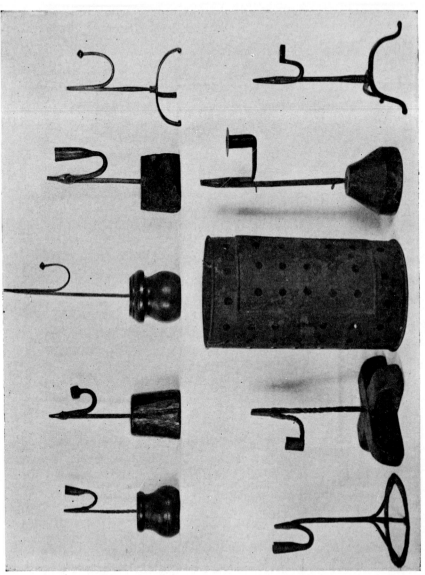

Plate 67   Rushlight holders and a rushlight shade   (Carleton Brown Collection)   (See page 108)

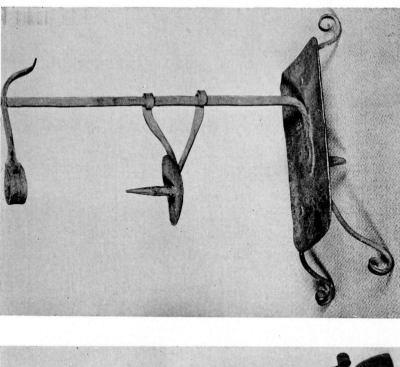

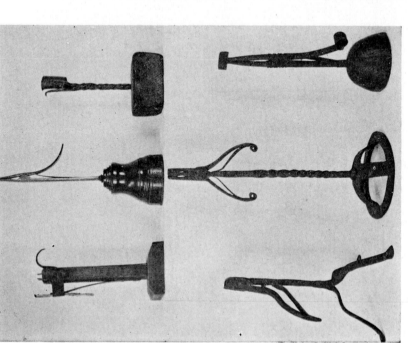

Plate 68 Left: Spring rushlight holders (Carleton Brown Collection). *Right:* Torch or flambeau holder (Julius Daniels Collection) (National Gallery of Art, Index of American Design) (See pages 108 & 111)

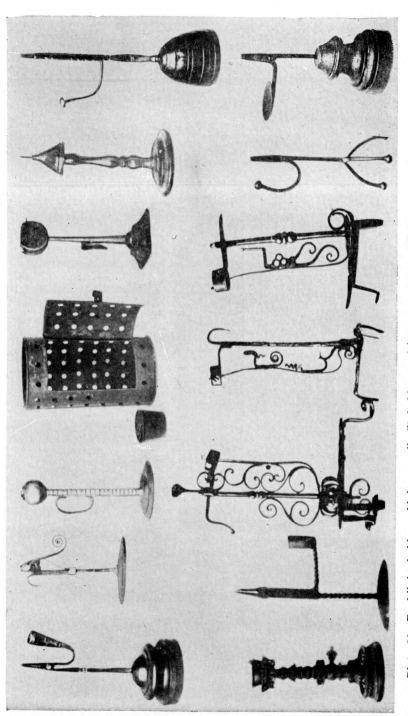

Plate 69 Rushlight holders, Alpine candle (?) holders and (top center) a rushlight screen with rush holder (From the Brown and the Science Museum Collections) (See pages 108 & 110)

Plate 70 Top. Two "toe" lamps. *Bottom:* Petticoat, whale oil, miner's, lard oil, etc lamps (Kenneth Mathews Collection)

Plate 71 Betty lamps (Carleton Brown Collection) (See page 33)

Plate 72 Two 17th century candlesticks and a later model. Frying pan type candle holder (Helen Brigham Hebard Collection) (See pages 112 & 114)

Rushlights, Tapers and Candles

Rushlights

Rushlights are candle-like lighting devices made by dipping the pith of the soft rush, *Juncus effusus*, once or more times in melted fat. The pith of these rushes resembles a pipe cleaner and is so soft that a strip of the hard outer cortex is needed to support it. They were usually a homemade product, in which case they were dipped or soaked in fat only once. However, rushlights supplied to the writer by a well-known firm of English candlemakers some years ago, had evidently been dipped several times as they were nearly three-eighths of an inch in diameter. These are better rushlights but they are more trouble to make. They burn longer but no better than rushes dipped once. Neither of the above will burn in a vertical position but if the dipping process is continued long enough they will. They then become rush-candles.

Rushlights may be older than true candles. Evidence is lacking on this. We know that the Romans used rush wicks in lamps and there is a Latin word *ellychnium* which is defined as: "a name given by the ancients to that sort of matter which served them for the wicks of their lamps... it was spongy and light and when properly prepared served for wicks, being very inflammable." (Rees Encyclopedia, vol. 12.) King Alfred's time candle probably had a rush wick and if it did, rushlights must have been used in England earlier than the ninth century, but it was not until 1788 that anyone described them in any detail and told how they were made. Gilbert White in his *Natural History of Selburne* called attention to their advantages, which seems to imply the use of rushlights was not common in all parts of England. White says that they should be gathered in the height of summer and kept in water until they were stripped of their outer coating, all but one narrow strip to hold the pith together. When dry they were dragged or dipped in "common kitchen grease or scummings." Six pounds of fat was enough to dip a pound of rushes, which would be a considerable number as they are so light. White also says: "a pound and a half of rushes will supply a family all the year round. A rushlight a little over two feet long will burn almost an hour." (Recent trials have confirmed this.)

Soft rushes have been found in various places in New England but none of them were as large as the English rushes in the rushlights furnished the writer. In Rockland, Maine, the plant grows in wet ground. It grows in clusters with no noticeable leaves and is best recognized by a cluster of blossoms on one side only, about six inches from the top. The cortex is easily removed if they are peeled at once, leaving a narrow strip about an eight of an inch or less to support the pith. They can be dipped in melted suet with a little candle grease added. But not too much, as the contraction of this harder material will cause the rush to curl. If you dip them many times until they are candle size, you will have an excellent candle which does not need to be snuffed.

William Cobbett (1766–1833), an Englishman who sometimes wrote under the highly appropriate name of Peter Porcupine, makes some interesting comments in his *Cottage Economy*. He is also worthy our notice because he published in this country, (1799) a short-lived magazine called *The Rushlight*. He wrote:

"We are not permitted to make candles ourselves, and if we were, they ought seldom to be used in a labourer's family. I was brought up by rushlight, and I do not find that I see less clearly than other people. My grandmother who lived to be ninety, never burnt a candle in her house in her life. I know that I never saw one there. She used to get meadow rushes when they had attained their full substance but were still green......You take off all the green skin except for about a fifth of the way around the pith. Thus it is a piece of pith with but a little strip of skin to hold it together.

"The rushes being thus prepared, grease is melted and put into something that is as long as the rushes are. They are put into the grease; soaked in it sufficiently; then taken out and laid in a piece of bark taken from a young tree."

"The rushes are carried about by hand; but to sit by, to work by or to go to bed by, they are fixed in stands made for the purpose. These have an iron part something like a pair of pliers to hold the rush, which is shifted forward as it burns. These rushes give a better light than a common dip candle and they cost next to nothing. If reading be your taste, you may read......as well by rushlight as you can by the light of taxed candles."

Rushlights are the oldest candle-like device to continue in use unchanged well into the nineteenth century. Henry Coleman of Salem, Massachusetts, (*European Life and Manners*; 1849) found them in the guest rooms of large county estates, where they were used as night lights, held in the large pierced sheet iron shields, as illustrated in Plate 69, top center.

Links

Walter Hough in Bulletin 141 of the Smithsonian Institution defines a link as follows: "A rope imbued with wax, resin or tar forming a rigid, though crude torch, which the English call a link." The Oxford Dictionary defines it as a rope soaked in pitch. A link is an improved torch and a flambeau, to be described later, is an improvement on a link. Links were widely used at night in English cities. There were link boys to carry them, and inverted cone-shaped link extinguishers were attached near the doors of great houses. Charles Dickens often mentions these. We have a single example of a link in the National Museum at Washington. It is made of coarse rope fibres dipped in rosin. It was found in Spain in 1892, where such torches were still being used by the railroad.

Flambeaux are described by Savary in his *Dictionnaire de Commerce* (1728) as rough candles with more than one wick, made with varying combinations of refined pitch, tallow, or wax. This is a seventeeth-century description, as Savary died in 1695. A better description is found in Rees' Encyclopedia (1829): "Flambeaux consist of four courses of hempen yarn wicks, half twisted, near an inch thick and three feet long. Wax is poured down these wicks and then the four are joined with a hot iron. Later more wax is poured on them until they weight from 1½ to 3 pounds." It seems probable that many of the tall candle-like "torches" depicted in the hands of tenth to seventeenth-century bearers are flambeaux. Fifteenth-century El Greco shows many of them.

The flambeaux used by royalty in Spain in the seventeenth century are described in the following quotation from *A Relation of a Voyage to Spain* (1679) by the Countess d'Aunoy.

The night the King was in Antocha we illuminated all our house with great flambeaux of white wax. They are longer than those used in Paris to light the coaches at night and a great deal dearer......When a lady goes to visit another at night, four pages come to receive her with smaller flambeaux, which are something larger than the wax candles enclosed in links, used in France.

Tapers

The term " taper " has meant different things at different times and places. Its first noted use in Saxon England was in 895. The Philips Dictionary of 1696 defines it as: " a long and large wax light in the form of a pyramid." This is a type with which we are unfamiliar. Pluche's *Encyclopedie* of 1732 describes and illustrates tapers as slender candles made in great lengths by a continuous process and this process has been used ever since. Modern dictionaries define " taper " as a small candle and this is a good general definition. Sometimes those made in great lengths are cut off to make small candles while others are cut to be used in the taper holders to be described later.

Candles

A candle may appear to be a very simple device but this is deceptive. If candles were as simple as they seem to be, they would have developed to their present state of near perfection much sooner than they did. All flame-type lighting devices are in effect miniature gas producers, as it is burning gas that feeds the flame. All but the simplest lamps have something to help gasify the oil, but candles require no outside help or attachments to accomplish this, starting with a solid fuel. They are complete in themselves.

Although candles have but two parts, the wick and the fat or wax, each of these must be suitably adapted and proportioned for the service it provides. The wick is far from simple. An eighteenth-century wick was made of twisted cotton, it stood up straight in the cool part of the flame and collected soot at the top, resulting in a dim light and a smoky flame until it was snuffed. In 1820, Cambaceres discovered that if the wick were braided instead of twisted, it would tend to curl out into the area of combustion and be snuffed automatically. This principle has been improved on in practice. Modern wicks are braided in a certain way so that they bend on the side on which the strands incline downward from the edge of the wick to the center. They tend to be flattish rather than round.

In the early part of the nineteenth century Chevreul and others developed methods for separating the better candle materials from tallow, suet and other natural fats. These methods produced stearine which is not greasy, which has a higher melting point and has less tendency to gutter. Although candles continued for some years to be made at home, and sometimes by travelling candlemakers, this practice was gradually superseded by factory-made products using better materials, machinery and other facilities for mass production. These were better candles than could be made from tallow and suet. However, candles continued to be made on the farm, as we read that a slaughtered ox furnished 80 pounds of suet, which in turn would make 300 candles, four to the pound. Town and city dwellers had to buy their candles.

Candle Making

Candles made at home were produced either by molding or dipping. They can be made one at a time by either method but it is not practical if any considerable number are to be made. The itinerant candlemaker molded them a hundred at a time and even the housewife dipped a dozen wicks at once. However if anyone wishes to make a candle at home today, just to learn how it was done, it is quite easy if a few rules are followed. They can be made from melted candle ends or from suet melted down in a double boiler or any combination of the two. There should ˙be a container for the melted fat at least as deep as the candles are long and it is better to put this in a pail of water held at about 130 degrees. The best temperature varies with the mixture. Wicks can be obtained from melted candles. If the fat is too hot the candle will build up very slowly. Give it time to harden after dipping. Turn off the gas or electricity and as the fat gradually cools, the candles will build up very quickly. The wick should be straightened after the first two dippings and when the job is finished, the lower end should be cut off square with a warm knife. The fat should be stirred occasionally as it cools more rapidly on the surface.

Other materials have been and are still used for making candles; paraffin and beeswax, the wax from the bayberry bush, and spermaceti from the head cavity of sperm whales. Paraffin is a petroleum product used for the cheapest candles. Bayberry candles are made from the berries of the wax myrtle that grows along the Atlantic coast. These are luxury items. It is often stated that they give off a fragrant odor while burning, but many people are unable to detect it. There is however a slight fragrance to the vapor rising from the wick just after it has been extinguished. Peter Kalm, the Swedish naturalist who visited this country in the first half of the eighteenth century, says: "...they grow (the berries) abundantly and look as if flour had been strewed upon them. They are gathered in the fall and thrown into a pot of boiling water...the wax floats and is skimmed off. When refined it has a rather transparent green color. This wax is dearer than tallow but cheaper than beeswax. Such candles do not bend easily nor melt in summer. They burn better and without smoke, yielding an agreeable smell when extinguished."

Spermaceti candles are the best candles of all and were formerly used as a standard for measurement of candle-power. Spermaceti is a translucent, slightly crystalline wax that vaporizes easily, so that there is never any accumulation of liquid in the cup at the base of the wick.

Since medieval times, beeswax candles have been preferred by the Catholic Church and by people who could afford them. This wax comes from the comb enclosing the honey and for practical reasons is mixed with other

104

Plate 73 Water lenses (Carleton Brown Collection) (See page 119)

Plate 74 Top: Sabbath or sabbath-type lamps (Carleton Brown Collection). *Bottom:* Two pewter lard oil lamps (Helen Brigham Hebard Collection) (See pages 55 & 84)

Plate 75 Float lamps (Carleton Brown Collection) (See page 11)

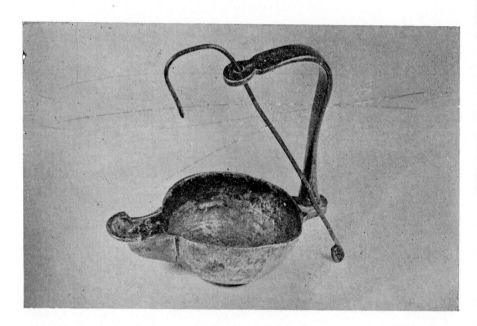

Plate 76   Top: Brass wick channel lamp from the Near East   (Kenneth Mathews Collection).   *Bottom:* Candle holder and lamp with hurricane shade (Kenneth Mathews Collection)   (See page 19)

Plate 77 A grisette and a professional candle mold with red pottery tubes marked "Wilcox" (Carleton Brown Collection) (See page 106)

Plate 78 American pottery lamps (Carleton Brown Collection) (See page 23)

Plate 79 American pottery lamps (Carleton Brown Collection) (See page 23)

Plate 80   Left: Candlemold and water bath. *Right:* A rushlight or splint holder   (Edwin B. Rollins Collection)   *Bottom:* Grisette for dipping rushes or tapers   (Helen Brigham Hebard Collection)   (See pages 106 & 108)

candle materials—but always within limits set by the Church and by the guilds. According to the best evidence we have, wax candles were formerly made by pouring the melted wax on the wick, as shown in 1732 by Pluche, and finished by rolling them on a flat table. There is no present evidence that the early wax candles were ever made by dipping although they could have been. If wax candles can be made in molds, no one has mentioned it. If this is possible, it must be a trade secret, as wax sticks very tightly to the surface against which it cools. Other waxes have been used in China and elsewhere but they have rarely been used in this country.

A torch, as we now understand it, is a device with a splint core, but in medieval times "torchis" were large wax candles. They are often mentioned in early church and guild records. Perhaps this is what Judge Samuel Sewall meant when he wrote in his diary in 1688: "I went to the funeral of Lady Andros, lychus illuminating the cloudy air. The church was made light with candles and torches." Evidently three different lighting devices are metioned here. We do not know the difference between "lychus" and torches, but we do know that the latter were once used in the Old South Church in Boston.

The value of candles—and candle ends, together with their peculiar status in the domestic economy of a twelfth-century English king's castle, is demonstrated by the following excerpt from the payroll of Henry II, who died in 1189.

> *Chancellor* · 5 shillings daily and one royal simnel (loaf of wheat bread) with 2 of drippings; 1 sectary of household wine; 1 wax candle and 40 candle ends.

Master of the scriptorium: 1 thick candle, 1 taper and 24 candle ends.

Stewards of the Bread: If he shall eat outside the king's house, 2 shillings and 10 pence daily.

Keeper of the dishes and the mazers: A double ration.

The Carter of the Great Kitchen: A double ration and for his horse, a proper allowance.

The Watchman. Double rations and 3½ pence and 4 candles. Of a morning, 2 loaves and a dish of meat and a gallon of beer.

The Washerwoman: Doubtfull.

The Watercarriers: A double ration, and if the King goes abroad, 1 penny to wring the King's clothes when he bathes. And 3 pence except on the three feast days of the year.

Candle Molds

A candle mold is a tapering tube with a hole for the wick at the smaller end. The other end flares out abruptly to form a shallow funnel, across which a rod is laid and to which the other end of the wick is tied. They are as old as the fourteenth century, as the following excerpt from the *Rules for Candlemakers* of Rouen for 1360 proves.

> None but those who have served their apprenticeship and passed the customary tests shall have in their shops either molds or tools (*ni moules ni ontils*) or make *chandelles a broque.*" (Ouin-Lacroix)

A *broque* is a thin rod, so we can assume that the latter type of candles were dipped, requiring neither molds nor tools for their production. Sieur de Brez, a fifteenth-century

106

French noblemen is commonly credited with the invention of candle molds but they evidently were used in Rouen before he was born.

The candle molds commonly seen today in museums and collections are made of tin and have from six to a dozen tubes for candles about nine inches long and three-quarters of an inch in diameter at the larger end. Few of these are likely to be older than 1750. The molds useds by the candlemakers of Rouen were probably made of lead or pewter cast around a suitable form. They may have been used in France for centuries but evidence of this is lacking both there and in England. Possibly then, as now, dipping was the cheapest process. A dozen or more candles could be dipped in less time than twelve wicks could be strung in the molds, the tallow poured, cooled and the candles pulled out. This latter process is not always easy as amateur candlemakers have discovered.

It is a fair assumption that molds for from six to twelve candles are for domestic use and the larger ones for the chandler. These are made for two hundred or more average-sized candles and are set in wooden frames. One of these for large candles is shown in Plate 65 together with others, including one of a cylindrical form. The combination of a mold fixed in a bath, Plate 80, top, is most practical. After pouring the hot fat into the molds, the candles can be cooled with cold water and when it is time to remove them, they can be loosened up by filling the tank with warm water. The lower plate illustrates at the left two unusually small molds, since the tubes are less than five inches tall. The tubes in the two-candle mold are about the same length as they extend nearly to the bottom of the base.

Holding Devices

for

Rushlights, Tapers and Candles

Mechanically there are three ways of holding anything; it can forced into something or onto something or be gripped by something. Rushlights and tapers have to be gripped, while candles are held by one of the other two methods.

Rush holders or rush stands or rushlight holders are necessary for burning dipped rushes because they have to be held at an angle as splints do, consequently many splint holders and most rush holders have taken the form of inverted pincers. The former can usually be distinguished as they are taller, heavier and have broader grips. Rushlight holders are made of hand-forged iron and no two of them are alike. Many of them are rather roughly made and have a simple joint, that is, the two parts are laid together and rivetted through the double thickness of metal. Others are more delicately designed, smoothly finished and have a joint like the one on scissors. The slight pressure required to hold a rush is usually provided by a counter-weight on the movable jaw. It may be a mass of iron or a candle socket. In other and more rare types, this pressure is exerted by a spring. See Plates 67, 68 and 69.

As noted earlier, there is no present evidence that rushlights were used on the Continent. No rushlight holders are illustrated in either D'Allemagne's *Histoire de Luminaire* or Von Benesch's *Das Beleuchtungswesen*. Nor are they mentioned in any of the detailed inventories of Essex (Mass.)

seventeenth-century estates or any other colonial records. If rushlight holders were ever used in America, cogent evidence of it is lacking. At present rushlight holders seem to come from England, Scotland and possibly Northern Ireland.

There is one other type of holder that has been called a rushlight holder but probably is not one. (Plate 66, lower right). The few that the author has seen or noted in illustrations are very much alike, which is not true of similar devices. They are about two feet tall with a flat base. The unusual feature is an inverted L-shaped grip evidently intended to hold something the size of a lead pencil in a vertical position. Neither splints nor rushlights will burn in this position but a torch of the link type would. A taper would also but the size of the utensil suggests that it was not made for domestic use. A loosely braided rope soaked in fat or pitch could be firmly held in the proper position and be drawn up as it burned. This is all speculation, but it is highly doubtful if these devices were made to hold either splints or rushlights.

Another rare type has a T-shaped grip that could hold a splint, a rushlight or a taper at any angle. Since these utensils seem to be individually designed it would be hazardous to say what this particular holder was intended for.

Taper Holders

Taper holders are relatively rare. They usually were made of brass and more rarely of wrought iron. This suggests that they were used mostly by the wealthier classes. They are a continental device. In England it is likely that they were used not for lighting but for warming the die and wax used in sealing letters. They were often made of

109

silver. See Plate 63, top row. There are two general types. One has a scissor-like grip but with the blades in the same plane. This is supported by a standard and a flat platform on legs. The taper is coiled around the standard and gripped by the blades. The second type is similar but the taper is drawn up through a short bell-mouthed tube, into which it fits tightly enough to hold it in place. The taper is usually coiled up in a helix under the tube but it can be coiled around the standard as shown. A New York collector has a rare " taper jack " with two jointed horizontal arms. This is a fine specimen of craftmanship and one can but wonder where and when it was made. See Plate 93.

Alpine Holders

There is another type of holder that has been called in America " Alpine " because it seems to be found only in Alpine countries. (See the illustration shown in the Glossary-Index.) It is questionable if such holders were originally intended for candles as they are unnecessarily complicated for that purpose. A simple one is illustrated in Plate 66 and there are many of them in the Von Benesch Collection that are lavishly ornate. If a simple pricket or socket-type candleholder would accommodate whatever kind of lighting device was in common use in those countries in the eighteenth century or earlier, there would seem to be no reason for the extra work required in making the Alpine type. One explanation might be that some torch-type " candle " was burned in these holders ; evidently something much larger than an ordinary candle. From the number and quality of the holders collected by Von Benesch, who was an Austrian, it is not only evident that they were popular in the Alpine countries but that they were cherished

110

possessions, involving a considerable expenditure of time, skill or money. We are so far from the countries where these were used and so unfamiliar with their common usage that it is futile to speculate on what they were intended to hold. (See also Plate 69.)

The device shown in Plate 68, right, is a rarity. It has both a pricket and an adjustable holding ring. This, too, came from one of the Alpine countries and the nature of the lighting device it was intended to hold is equally in doubt.

Fig. 8. Sketch of a lamp by DaVinci, c. 1500

III

Candlesticks and Holders

It is reasonable to assume that devices to hold candles are nearly as old as candles themselves; the word "candelabrum" may be older but according to Varro, this was used to hold burning ropes. In later Roman times the word meant a lamp holder or stand but that was not what the device was originally intended for. Any candle-like lights that the Romans may have used were carried in the hand. Apuleus does not definitely state this, but he implies it. If there were holders for these lights, nothing of the sort has been so identified among the many objects excavated at Pompeii and Herculaneum. Classical type torch holders like the one carried by the Statue of Liberty and those depicted on Greek vases, should not be confused with either candle-holders or candelabra.

Candleholders, strictly speaking, include any utensil intended to hold a candle, but the term is commonly applied to portable types with a short pedestal and a wide saucer base with a finger grip. The skillet type shown in Plate 72 may be one of the oldest. One of these was found several feet below the surface, when the site of the now restored Aptuxet Trading Post at Bourne on Cape Cod was excavated in 1930. This post was established by the Pilgrims in 1626 and was not abandoned until 1660. It could have been taken in trade with the Dutch in New Amsterdam or it may have been brought from Holland where the Pilgrims lived for eleven years. Artists of the Dutch School

Plate 81   Chafing balls, five inches in diameter   (Kenneth Mathews Collection)
(See page 120)

Plate 82 Glass and tin lamps for drop burners (Carleton Brown Collection)

Plate 83 Rolling lamp (*center*) and chafing balls. The one at the upper right could be either a lamp or an incense burner (Carleton Brown Collection) (See page 120)

Plate 84 Top: Betty on wooden stand and Betty on tidy top. *Bottom:* Betty
lamps with supports or standards (Carleton Brown Collection) (See page 33)

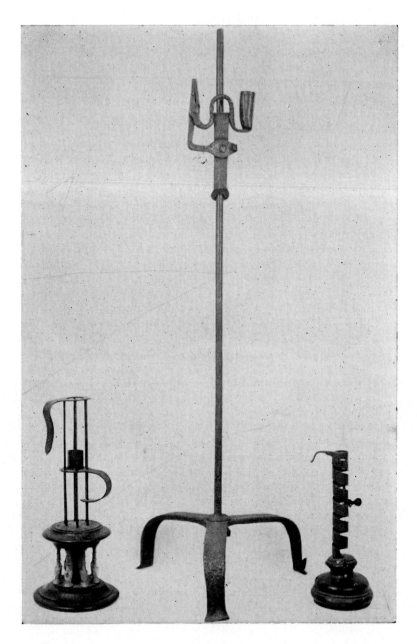

Plate 85 A tall splint or rushlight combination holder, a bird cage candleholder and a spiral candleholder (Carleton Brown Collection) (See pages 108 & 116)

Plate 86   Top: Marked Betty lamp   (Kenneth Mathews Collection). *Bottom:* Betty lamps with ornamental bails and a trammel (Carleton Brown Collection) (See page 33)

Plate 87 Top: Two pickwicks. *Bottom:* A spill planer for lighting cigars
(Hazel Brown Collection) (See page 117)

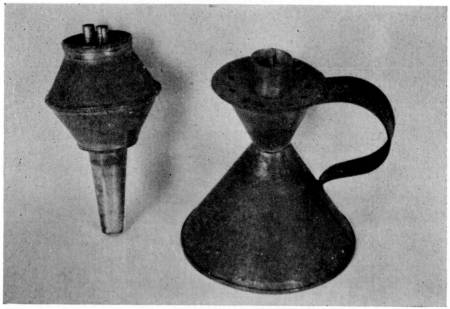

Plate 88 A sanding lamp. The peg lamp lifts out so that the sand in the base can be used as a blotter (Carleton Brown Collection) (See page 51)

show candleholders of this this type in their paintings. Regardless of the country of its origin, this is one colonial lighting device that can be definitely dated as a seventeenth-century piece.

Candlesticks and candleholders have been discussed so frequently in books on silver, glass, brass and pottery and so well illustrated in such magazines as *Antiques*, that only their technical aspects need be considered here. They are made of so many different materials, styled in so many periods and patterns and are so readily available that use for a pair can be found in any home, for decorative purposes, for practical use on the dining table or for an emergency. Technically there are but two types of candle-holding devices—the pricket and the socket types. The former is commonly believed to be the older but we know too little about early candles and candleholders to be sure.

Prickets

Prickets hold the candle on a sharp spike. They are at least as old as the fifth or sixth century A.D. and their simplicity and adaptability to any size candle is evidence of their priority. They are found throughout Europe, and in China and Japan. Walter Hough in *Bulletin 141* says: " The surviving examples are ecclesiastical and large, for placing on altars." F. W. Robins in *The Story of the Lamp and the Candle* agrees but finds others that are evidently the work of the village smith. A few small prickets may be seen in private collections and in museums but these are rare as are hand-forged models. See Plate 66, bottom row.

Candlesticks

Candlesticks could be defined roughly as tall candleholders, but their height is not their distinctive feature; it is their design, which makes no provision for an efficient drip catcher. For the past three hundred years they have not been designed primarily as portable lighting devices, however much they may have been so used earlier. They were intended as moveable lights for use on a table or mantel. Such lights do not need a large drip catcher such as that provided on a bedroom candleholder. Prior to the fifteenth century, if we can judge by the few pictures we have, the only drip catcher was a heavy base but as time went on, this feature developed as shown on page 115. The left hand fifteenth-century model has no separate drip catcher but the one at the right has one. The sixteenth-century type has a short standard and requires none, but the three dated " c. 1600 " and the others from this century show how the drip catcher rises from the base to a more practical position just below the candle socket and finally forms a small convex part at the very top. See also Plate 72.

Candlesticks were usually made of cast metal and candleholders of sheet metal, the former being cheaper than the latter until power rolling mills were built in the eighteenth century. John Stow in his *Survey of London* (1548) mentions the street where brass candlesticks were being turned from the rough castings on pole lathes, " with a horrid scrating sound." Since Stow's time there has been little technical improvement in candlesticks. The seventeenth-century models shown in Plate 72 have only a hole in the socket for ejecting the candle end but sometime later a piston-type push out extending down to the hollow base was invented. The specimen in the middle may have this, but we cannot be sure since we cannot see the inside of the base.

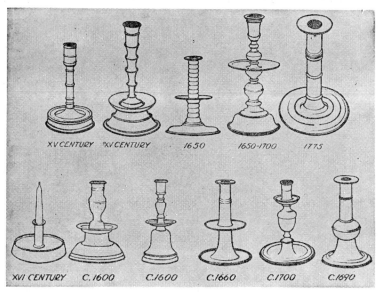

Fig. 9. The development of candlesticks

Candleholders

Candlesticks are not grouped by technical differences. Candleholders, however, are found in a variety of functional forms. There are bedroom types, handsome silver models with chimneys or shades, hogscrapers and sticking tommies. There are candelabra, chandeliers and sconces. Another group is adapted to the special requirements of different trades, such as bakers, cobblers, vintners and others. A third group—and it is quite large—contains specimens no one has been able to identify, although there have been many guesses. The number and variety of these make it impossible to discuss candleholders fully within the limits of this book. See Plate 7. There are two varieties, however, that should be mentioned. They are commonly called candleholders although they have slight provision for catching the drip. These are wire candleholders. There are two kinds, each with its own name.

A "wyre" candleholder is mentioned in a seventeenth-century Essex County record. We now know of only two kinds, the spiral and the birdcage types. See Plates 66 and 85 and others in group pictures. Spiral candleholders could have been easily made by the village blacksmith. Some are quite heavy. The birdcage type, which is more delicate and better adapted for home use, has been called a barn candleholder, as the vertical wires give some protection to the flame, but it is doubtful if they were made for this purpose. They are not particularly stable or suited for rough usage. Both have candle lifts. One is adjusted by a tab on the socket which projects between the spirals. In the other, the socket slides on the vertical wires. In other kinds of candleholders the candle lift slides in a slot in the candle tube and is held in place either by friction or by a series of notches.

There are also floor models and candlestands. For these the reader is referred to Nutting's *Furniture Treasury*, where many types are illustrated.

Spring candlesticks or holders have a spiral spring in the candle tube which forces the candle against a flange at the top of the tube. A device of this kind is necessary whenever the position of the flame must be maintained at a given point as in carriage lamps and table models with concave or parabolic reflectors. They are in no wise modern as the two in the picture of the seventeenth century *ferblantier* (page 41) proves. They are illustrated

116

and described in Abbe Pluche's *Encyclobedie* of 1732. The Abbe calls them *flambeaux d' elude,* and for the first time discusses the distribution of light.

"It is not difficult to increase the amount of light from a candle. One way is to suspend a clear glass globe of water in front of it. Another is to use a shade, which should be so tipped that the rays of light will be concentrated on the work to be performed. The candle tube should be slanted at an angle of from 45 to 60 degrees from the horizontal. The inside of the shade or reflector should be lined with paper having a dull finish but this is dangerous. A copper shade can be given a coating of white lead, which is easily renewed or plated with quick-silver, which soon oxydizes leaving a non-reflecting surface.

Candle Accessories

Snuffers for candles and pickwicks for lamps are very old. "Snuff dishes" are mentioned in the *Book of Exodus.* The oldest known snuffers were like small scissors or pincers but when the carbonized part of the wick was cut off, it often fell where it was not wanted, so a small box was added to the device to catch it. The older ones have a half box on each blade. Sometimes there was a spike to uncurl the wick if necessay before cutting it off. A douter is a rare extinguisher of the pincer type with a small disc on each jaw. A few specimens have a snuff box attached. They are probably older than the scissors type as the first-noted use of the word was in 1526. Pickwicks are what the name indicates. They may be simply a piece of wire such as we find attached to lucernas or the wire may be

117

set into a turned base with a cover as in Plate 87.

The conical extinguishers for links, flambeaux and candles are probably very old since they provide the simplest and most efficient way of "putting out" a light. They are commonly made of sheet iron, brass or tin. These are strictly functional but rare decorated types are made of pottery and porcelain in the form of human figures.

Savealls

A saveall is a device for burning the last inch of a candle. In the sixteenth century and later, in England, hard fats sold for more than lean meat on account of the demand for candle grease. A common form of saveall is a small pan with a pin on which the candle end is fixed. The pan has a shank which can be set into the candle socket. Instructions for their use dated 1642 state: "Heat the pin of a saveall and thrust it into the candle end and so set it upon a candlestick." In an inventory of the goods in a shop owned by William Wharton of Salem, dated December 1, 1677, several models are listed. There are wooden, brass, "second sort" and "5 best savealls at 2 shillings and 4 pence each." There must have been considerable demand for these penny saving devices. Webster's Dictionary (1880) defines a saveall as "A small pan or a short cylinder of wood or stone with a pin at the top." These stone and wooden models must be quite rare today. Walter Hough (*Bulletin 141*) illustrates in (his) Plate 38 three types without the central pin, the candle end being held in short springs. One was purchased in France in 1892, where they are appropriately called *brule toutes*. At about the same time an English *Army and Navy Frice List* for 1895 has: "Candle savealls, white, 4½d. each." See top portion of Plate 66.

Water Lenses, Chafing Balls and Rolling Lamps

Water lenses or refractors are at least as old as the sixteenth century and the fact that they have been used so long by lacemakers, cobblers and others testifies to their practical value. This has been demonstrated by Mr. W. O'Dea of the London Science Museum using a one candle power electric lamp. The concentration of light over the working area is evident. In another demonstration cited in *The Rushlight* (see bibliography), " A water-filled globe using the light of a single candle, projected a beam of light on the back wall of the room......The eye of a needle is magnified many times and although the candle may flicker, the focussed beam will be quite constant."

Present information indicates that these globes were more popular in Continental Europe than in England and that they were products of the Bohemian glass blowers. Von Benesch, who was an Austrian, illustrates them, while D'Allemagne, a Frenchman, does not. Suspension types are the most common but there are others that are self sustaining, being flask-shaped with a flat bottom, frequently consisting of small globes mounted on wooden standards. See Plate 73. Lacemakers and cobblers have been mentioned as users of water lenses but there must have been others. We now uncertainly assume that cobblers did not work in groups as lacemakers did and that single globes were used more in shops than *ateliers* but this is a rash assumption, as some of the four-globe assemblies seem too heavy and clumsy for lacemakers. For additional discussion and pictures see *Antiques* for October 1949 and January 1955.

Chafing Balls and Rolling Lamps

Chafing balls are not lighting devices and do not properly come within the scope of this book but lamp collectors buy them because they are so much like rolling lamps. See Plates 81 and 83. Chafing balls are heaters. In the *Connoiseur* for January, 1940, there is a scholarly, well-documented and illustrated article on these hand warmers by Charles R. Beard. As the above English publication is not on file in many libraries, a short resumé is given here.

Mr. Beard evidently believes, but does not insist, that all these hollow spheres, made of embossed or pierced metal with a heater or lamp suspended on gimbals, regardless of size, are chafing balls or hand warmers. They come from Venice, Cairo and China and are at least as old as the thirteenth-century. They vary in size from three to nine inches in diameter. Those illustrated are usually sixteenth-century pieces. Anyone reading the above article and seeing the pictures cannot fail to be impressed by the author's conclusion, which is, that there is no such thing as a rolling lamp. He does not definitely say this but he implies it. There is however documentary evidence to the contrary.

In Desagulier's (Natural) *Philosophy* published in 1774, there is an engraving of a rolling lamp and it is so called in the caption. See *The Rushlight*, September, 1940. There is one other bit of evidence. A former member of the Rushlight Club who had lived in India, told the author that she had seen rolling lamps used in that country. On certain occasions they were rolled and raced down a suitable slope, making a pretty picture as they twinkled down the hill.

It is the author's tentative opinion that the larger balls are lamps and the smaller ones chafing balls. Those having heating rather than lighting devices or provision for hanging them around the neck, certainly are the latter. The immediately obvious difference, however, is their size. Those with diameters of approximately five inches are identified by the details of their construction. Spheres over five inches are probably rolling lamps unless there is something about them to deny it.

Mr. Beard says that a chafing ball is listed in the inventory of a fifteenth-century English king's estate. This did not necessarily have a gimbal suspension for the heater. A century later this might have happened, as Dr. Cardan, the inventor or at least the demonstrator of this device was called to Scotland to treat Archbishop Hamilton's asthma.

Fig. 10. A 16th century scholar (See page 119 "Water Lenses")

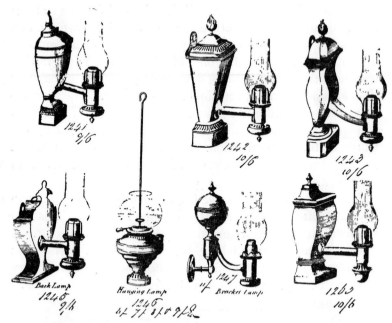

Fig. 11. From an old catalog (c. 1820) at the Essex Institute

Plate 89 An ornate spout lamp and a two-man Austrian plane for birch splints (Carleton Brown Collection) (See page 29)

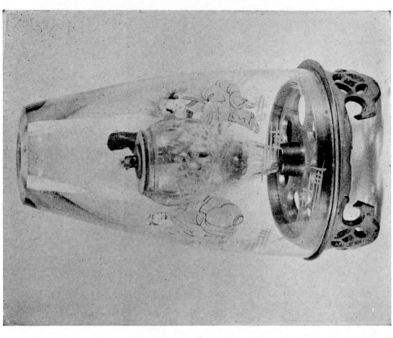

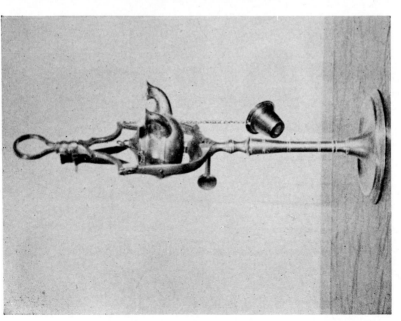

Plate 90 Left: Lucerna with adjustment for oil level. *Right* Chinese opium smoker's lamp (Kenneth Mathews Collection). (See page 30)

Plate 91 Left: Canting lamp with reflector *Right* Crusie on stand (Carleton Brown Collection) (See pages 16 & 53)

Plate 92 Taper holder (Howard Stone Collection) (See page 110)

Plate 93 Jointed taper holder (Miner Cooper Collection) (See page 110)

Plate 94 Time lamps (Carleton Brown Collection) (See page 40)

Plate 95 Blown glass lamps (Hazel Brown Collection)

Plate 96 Hitchcock lamps showing two types of blowers and two models with chimneys (Carleton Brown Collection)

References

The best books on the history of domestic illumination are listed below. Unfortunately, all of them are now out of print. Those marked with an asterisk contain relatively little about common lighting devices.

"Colonial Lighting," by Arthur H. Hayward.
"Heating and Lighting Utensils," by Walter Hough. (Bulletin number 141 of the U.S. National Museum)
"Artificial Lighting in America, 1830—1860," by C. Malcolm Watkins. (Publication number 4080 of the Smithsonian Institution)
"Darkness Into Daylight," by W. T. O'Dea. (Published by the Science Museum, London)
"Das Beleuchtungswesen," by Von Benesch.
* "Histoire du Luminaire, by D'Allemagne.
"The Story of the Lamp," by F. W. Robins. (Also concerns the candle)
"The House of Derr," by J. F. Spear. (Concerns Betty lamps)
* "Encyclopedie du Luminaire," by Gabriel Henriot. (A six-volume work)
"Old West Surrey," by Gertrude Jekyll. (Concerns rushlights)
"Cottage Economy," by Peter Cobbett. (Concerns rushlights)

"Rushlight" Magazine References

Information contained in the following articles was used by the author in the compilation of this book. All of these articles were printed originally in the "Rushlight" magazine, published by the Rushlight Club in Boston, Massachusetts. Issue and page numbers are given below.

"Antiques" Magazine References

All of the following articles on the history of domestic lighting were written by members of the RUSHLIGHT CLUB and
were published in the "Antiques" magazine. Issue and page
numbers are given below.

Illustrated Glossary-Index

The definitions given below have been adapted from *A Dictionary of Old Lamps and Other Lighting Devices*, written, published and copyrighted by Leroy Thwing and Julius Daniels, in 1952. The sketches are by Alfred Smith. Permission to reprint has been secured from the copyright holders.

The first glossary of the terms used in any branch of collecting is unavoidably incomplete and without universal acceptance. Objects have different names in different places. In the past, lamps seem to have had no common descriptive names, and the names found in early 19th century catalogs are not the names used by collectors today. The present attempt to improve and stabilize this condition is based on the terminology commonly accepted by the Rushlight Club of Boston, which is, to the best of our knowledge, the only group in the United States dedicated to the study of the history of domestic illumination.

— The Publishers

ALCOHOL, 59

ALPINE CANDLEHOLDERS, *see* CANDLEHOLDERS.

ARGAND BURNERS, 75

ARGAND LAMPS, 71

>These lamps have tubular wicks, invented by Argand in 1784, and fountain feed oil systems. Lamps with different feed systems have specific names such as: ASTRAL, SINUMBRA, SOLAR, CARCEL, etc.

ASTRAL LAMPS, 75

>These lamps have an Argand burner and an axially-located oil font. They are identified by the air holes around the base of the font. Mantle-arm lamps are erroneously called astral lamps.

BALLS, CHAFING, 119

BAYBERRY CANDLES, *see* CANDLES, BAYBERRY.

BENZENE, 61

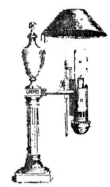

Argand Lamp

Astral Lamp

Betty Lamp

Burning Fluid Lamp

Candle Bracket

BETTY LAMPS, 33

This name is commonly given to certain flat, wick-support lamps. They are usually oval-, heart-, or pear-shaped, not over one and one-half inches deep, with a cover and a half-bail. While the word "Betty" is capitalized, there appears to be no etymological justification for this. *See also* IPSWICH BETTY.

BULL'S-EYE LAMPS, *see* LENS LAMPS.

BULL'S-EYE LANTERNS, *see* LENS LAMPS.

BURNERS, *see* names of specific burners.

BURNING FLUID, 59

BURNING FLUID LAMPS 59

Lamps with divergent or long wick tubes burning a mixture of alcohol and turpentine.

CAMPHENE, 59

Freshly distilled turpentine. Lamps burning this illuminant were called Vesta lamps in England. Burning fluid lamps with divergent tapered wick tubes are incorrectly called camphene lamps.

CANDELABRA, 115

Multiple socket candlesticks.

CANDLE ACCESSORIES, 117

CANDLE BEAMS, 115

A simple chandelier for candles in the form of an inverted "T". Commonly made of wood but also of iron.

CANDLE BRACKETS

Wall devices for candles. May be shaped like a "J" or have arms, rigid or jointed.

CANDLE LAMPS, *see* FAIRY LAMPS.

CANDLE MAKING, 103

CANDLE MOLDS, 106

CANDLE STANDS, 116

Iron or wooden floor stands with arms for candle sockets. Often adjustable for height by various mechanical devices, such as ratchets, wedges or screws. Also small tables for candlesticks.

CANDLEHOLDERS,

Portable devices equipped with a saucer base and a thumb or finger ring grip.

128

CANDLEHOLDERS, ALPINE, 110

These are called candleholders for lack of a more accurate term. It is doubtful if they were originally made to hold candles as the hole is too large and even the simplest of them was more difficult to make than the socket type. They would seem to be better adapted to hold a fabricated torch or link.

CANDLEHOLDERS, SPRING, 116

In these devices the candle is held in a tube with a hole for the wick at the top. As the candle burns it is forced upward by a spring. This device is at least as old as 1735.

CANDLEHOLDERS, STICKING TOMMY, 115 & Plate 7, item 42.

Also called miner's candleholders. These are equipped with one or more sharp points which can be set into cracks or thrust into beams.

CANDLEHOLDERS, WIRE, 116

These have had various unsubstantiated names. They are mentioned in 17th century Essex County records. The candle lift slides on two or more vertical wires.

CANDLES, 102

Candles in their present form—a small wick and a thick coating of fat—are not much older than 500 A.D.

CANDLES, BAYBERRY, 104

These are made from the berries of the wax myrtle bush which grows along the northeast coast of the United States and elsewhere. They are supposed to emit a fragrant odor while burning.

CANDLES, RUSH, see RUSHLIGHTS.

CANDLESTICKS, 114

Tall devices usually with a convex base for use on a table or mantel.

CANDLEWOOD TORCHES, *see* TORCHES.

CANTING LAMPS, 53

These are pivotted lamps so balanced that as the oil is consumed, the lamp cants or tips, causing the oil to flow into the wick end of the font.

CAPE COD LAMPS, 31

CARCEL LAMPS, 78

CARDAN'S LAMPS, 38

CHAFING BALLS, 119

Candleholder, Alpine

Candleholder, Alpine

Candleholder, Spiral

Candleholder, Wire

Candleholder, Wire

Canting Lamp

Convent Lamp

Crusie, Covered

CHRISTMAS LIGHTS, *see* FLOAT LAMPS.

CLASSICAL LAMPS, 2

CLOCK LAMPS, 40

COAL OIL LAMPS, 88

COBBLERS' LAMPS, *see* LACEMAKERS' LAMPS.

CONVENT LAMPS, 37

Tall pewter lamps with a wick support.

CRASSETS, 21

CRESSETS, 7

CRUSIES, 16, 19

There are both single and double crusies. They are usually pear-shaped, with a half-bail for suspension. Double crusies, or Phoebe lamps, have a lower pan to catch the drip and also a toothed arm to slant the upper pan. The covered crusie shown in the sketch is a rare type. It is made of wrought iron, has a deep, narrow wick slot and a cover. There is no indication that it ever had a wick tube or support.

DIACON LAMPS, 78

English or American models of the French Carcel lamp, which has a spring-driven pump to deliver oil to the top of the wick.

DOUTERS, 117

Scissor-like devices with two discs at the ends, between which the wick of a candle is pinched to snuff or extinguish it.

DROP BURNERS, 44

A drop burner is a vertical wick tube set in a burner plate. It drops into or onto the top of a hand-blown glass lamp.

FAIRY LAMPS, Plate 18, lower right

Candle lamps or night lamps with glass base and shade. Burns a thick short candle with a rush wick. Made by Price and Company of London until recently.

FLAMBEAUX, 100

Outdoor lighting devices, between a torch and a candle. In England, a link.

FLEMISH SPOUT LAMPS, 31

Sheet brass single-spout lamps on a standard with sand-weighted base. Usually has a suspension tab at the top, with the conical base flattened on that side. So named because they are shown as details in paintings of the Flemish school.

FLOAT LAMPS, 11
One of the oldest types of lamps ; as old as King Tut-Ankh-Amen. The wick is floated on the surface of the oil by a cork float or otherwise. Sanctuary lamps, Christmas lights, night lights, etc. are all float lamps.

FLUID, BURNING, 59

FLUID LAMPS, 59
Same as burning fluid lamps.

GASOLENE, 62

GIMBAL LAMPS
Ship's cabin lamps ; whale oil lamps hung in double trunnions or gimbals and weighted to hang or set vertically.

GIRANDOLE
A wall bracket candleholder particularly for the sides of mirrors, etc.

GREASE LAMPS, 16
Any kind of grease-burning lamp.

GRISETTES, Plates 77 & 80
Boat-shaped iron pans, used to hold the melted fat through which rushlights and tapers are drawn.

HANUKKAH LAMPS, 83
Jewish festival lamps, used in celebrating the feast of that name. Made of all common metals ; has eight oil fonts or candle holders, one for each day of the feast and one from which the others are lighted. This eighth lamp or candle is called the *shamash* or server.

HITCHCOCK LAMPS, 89
Kerosene lamps with spring-driven blower, designed to burn without a chimney.

HOLDING DEVICES, 108

HURRICANE GLASS, Plate 76
A tall cylindrical or barrel-shaped glass, put around a candlestick to protect the flame from drafts. A hurricane shade is a similar device attached to a wall candle bracket or candleholder.

IPSWICH BETTY, Plate 12
A name sometimes applied to Betty lamps on a standard or a tidy top. Such lamps are supposed to have been made in the town of Ipswich. *See also* TIDY TOPS.

Crusie, Double

Crusie, Double

Crusie, Single

Flemish Spout Lamp

Float Lamp

Grisette

Kettle Lamp

Kettle Lamp

KEROSENE LAMPS, 88

KETTLE LAMPS, 38

Wick tube lamps with font hung on trunnions. A Pennsylvania Dutch type of lamp.

KINNEAR PATENT LAMP, 64

LACEMAKERS' LAMPS

Blown glass lamps for drop burners. Also any small blown glass lamp such as a spark lamp. Cobblers' lamps are similar but larger and heavier.

LAMPS, *see* names of specific lamps.

LANTERNS, 86 & Plate 19

These vary greatly according to their shape and purpose. There are too many varieties to describe or illustrate here at any length.

LARD OIL LAMPS, 55

All lamps designed to burn lard oil (or lard?). Can be identified by the long copper or tin plates attached to the burner and extending downward to conduct the heat from the flame to the oil.

LENS LAMPS, 54

Pewter whale oil lamps with one, two or four planoconvex lenses to concentrate the light. A 19th century policeman's bull's-eye lantern is essentially a lens lamp.

LENSES, WATER, 119

LIGHTWOOD, 8

LINKS, 100

The English name for flambeaux or torches.

LUCERNAS, 30

Cast brass spout lamps used in Mediterranean countries until recently. Usually have three spouts with font adjustable for height on a vertical standard.

LUSTRES

Candelabra with glass prisms or pendants.

MANTEL-ARM LAMPS, 77

Argand lamps with one or two burners on arms projecting from the font. Made in England and France ; finished in natural or bronzed brass, often in sets of three, for the mantel. Erroneously called astral lamps.

MEDIEVAL LIGHTING, 9

MENORAH, 80

The great golden " candlestick " described in the Book of Exodus and portrayed on the Arch of Titus. It is not a candlestick but a lamp with seven fonts.

MILES PATENT LAMPS, 48

MINERS' CANDLEHOLDER, *see* **CANDLEHOLDERS, STICKING TOMMY.**

MODERATOR LAMPS, 77

Argand-type lamps popular from 1846 to 1865. The base is usually a large pottery vase or oil container. These handsome lamps may be identified by the large flat key used to compress the spring which forced oil up to the burner. There is also a button wick turn-up.

MOLDS, CANDLE, 106

NIGHT LAMPS, *see* **FAIRY LAMPS.**

NIGHT LIGHTS, 14

Originally these were simple glass float lamps, but by the 19th century various types were popular. The candle used was short and thick, with a rush wick.

NURSERY LAMPS, Plate 10

These lamps are a combination of a dark lantern, night light, heater for milk or shaving water, and candlestick, with a base containing flint, steel and tinder.

OIL LAMPS, *see* **LARD OIL LAMPS and WHALE OIL LAMPS.**

OLEOSTATIC LAMPS, 79

PAN LAMPS, 16

As a type these are the oldest lamps known. The sandstone lamp (a) is about 20,000 years old. This and all other pan lamps are not over half an inch deep. The moss or flaxen wick rests on the bottom ; in (c) and (d) near the narrow end. Lamp (b) is a pan lamp but if it had a drip pan it could be called a crusie. These lamps are commonly made of wrought iron or cast iron but also of copper and brass. A common Swiss type has two iron pans sliding on a rod with tripod base.

PARAGON LAMPS, 62

PASTORS' LAMPS, *see* **RABBIS' LAMPS**

PATENT LAMPS, 63

PATENT LAMPS, KINNEAR, 64

PATENT LAMPS, MILES, 48

Lens Lamp

Mantle Arm Lamp

Pan Lamp (a)

Pan Lamp (b)

Pan Lamp (c)

Pan Lamp (d)

Peg Lamp

Peg Lamp

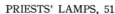

Petticoat Lamp

Pig Lamp

134

RUSHLIGHTS, 97
> Tapers having a rush wick, dipped once or more in hot fat. Rush candles are dipped many times until they are the size of a regular candle.

RUSHLIGHTS, HOLDING DEVICES, 108
> Rushlight holders are also called rush stands. They have an inverted pincer device for holding rushlights. See sketch.

SABBATH LAMPS, 84
> Jewish lamps lighted on Friday evenings. They have six or eight radial crusie-type fonts and a drip catcher. Usually made of brass, but also of copper, pewter and (rarely) silver.

SANCTUARY LAMPS, 12
> Cup- or vase-shaped float lamps. May be made of glass or metal. A hanging lamp used near the altar in early Christian churches.

SAUCER LAMPS, 17
> Shallow grease lamps ; pan lamps.

SAVEALLS, 118
> Peg-type candle prickets for burning the last inch of a candle.

SCONCE, 115
> A wall holder with a reflector, usually for candles, less frequently for lamps.

SHIP'S CABIN LAMPS, *see* GIMBAL LAMPS

SIMPLE LAMPS, 11

SINUMBRA LAMPS, 76
> Improved astral lamps invented in 1820. They have a large ring-shaped font of such cross section, and so located with respect to the flame, as to cast as little shadow as possible.

SNUFFERS, 117
> Scissor-like devices that cut off and catch the charred end of a candlewick.

SOLAR LAMPS, 76
> Astral lamps with a flame attenuator. This is a plate with a half-inch hole located just above the wick. Made by Cornelius & Co.

SPARK LAMPS,
> Small blown-glass lamps with a drop burner or possibly

Pump Lamp

Rabbis' Lamp

Rumford Lamp

Rushlight Holder

135

Splint Holder

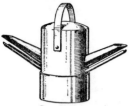

Spout Lamp

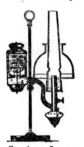

Student Lamp

Taper Holder

a whale oil burner, giving only a spark of light.

SPIRIT LAMPS, *see* VAPOR LAMPS

SPIRITS OF TURPENTINE, *see* CAMPHENE

SPLINT HOLDERS, 5

Holders for candlewood or splints. These are found in a variety of forms. A common type has two thin slightly diverging blades. Others are like heavy rushlight holders. Birch splints may be held in the mouth of a clay figure or across the arms of a forging or again in devices like miniature andirons or cob-irons.

SPLINTS, 3

SPOUT LAMPS, 29

All lamps having a spout-type wick tube, such as a Cape Cod lamp, a Flemish lamp or a lucerna.

SPOUT LAMPS, FLEMISH, 31

SPRING CANDLE HOLDERS, *see* CANDLEHOLDERS, SPRING.

STICKING TOMMY, *see* CANDLEHOLDERS.

STUDENT LAMPS

A Victorian adaptation of Argand's original lamp. The older ones are brass; the more recent (c.1890) nickel plate. See sketch.

SWOPE PATENT LAMPS, 65

TAPERS, 101

At different times and places this word has meant many different things. Today it usually means either a small wax candle or a small candle made in continuous lengths and burned in taper holders or wound into cones or pyramids and pulled off as required.

TAPERS, HOLDING DEVICES, 109

These holders are also called jacks, reels and winders. Taper holders or jacks grip the taper between horizontal pincers at the top of a support on a three- or four-legged base. There is no provision for holding tapers of any length as there is in reels and winders. Here the taper is wound on a reel or drum and is unwound and pulled up through a grip as needed. The most common taper winders were made of silver.

TESTS ON WHALE OIL BURNERS, 50

TIDY TOPS, Plate 12, item 3 & plate 84

Stands or holders for Betty Lamps, usually made of tin.

TIME LAMPS, 40
Lamps marked to show the time according to the level of the oil. The usual type is a Cardan glass and pewter lamp, twelve inches or more in height.

TORCHES, 3
A torch has a little tar, pitch or fat and a very large wick. A candlewood torch has its own pitch. The purpose of fat, etc., on a torch or flambeau is to help burn the wick, whereas in a candle the purpose of the wick is to help burn the fat.

TURPENTINE, *see* **CAMPHENE.**

TWIN-TUBE BURNERS, 47

VAPOR LAMPS, 62
Also called spirit lamps. Lamps without visible wicks, burning volatile fluids such as naphtha or gasolene.

VERTICAL WICK TUBE LAMPS, 43

VESTA LAMPS, 62
English Argand lamps designed to burn camphene or spirits of turpentine.

WATER LENSES, 119

WEDDING LAMPS, Plate 18, upper right
Kerosene lamps with two burners on the same font.

WHALE OIL BURNERS, 50
Wick tube burners having a threaded wick plate and twin tubes.

WHALE OIL LAMPS, 49
Lamps, as shown in the sketch, made of tin, brass, pewter, silver or glass.

WICK CHANNEL LAMPS, 19

WICK SUPPORT LAMPS, 16, 33, 37
Lamps having a half-tube supporting the wick. Convent lamps belong in this group.

WICK TUBE LAMPS, 43

WIRE CANDLE HOLDERS, *see* **CANDLEHOLDERS, WIRE**

WITCH LAMPS, 22
Heavy cast iron lamps of the crusie type ; may not have a cover. So named because such lamps were supposed to have been used in the Salem jail where those accused of being witches were confined. It is also claimed that

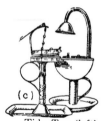
Tidy Top (left)
Swope Patent Lamp (right)

Trunnion Lamp

Whale Oil Lamp

Witch Lamp

such lamps were used in machine shops and foundries in the United States in 1860 and much earlier in England.

WOOD-BURNING UTENSILS,